Law Firm Librarianship

CHANDOS
INFORMATION PROFESSIONAL SERIES

Series Editor: Ruth Rikowski
(Email: Rikowskigr@aol.com)

Chandos' new series of books is aimed at the busy information professional. They have been specially commissioned to provide the reader with an authoritative view of current thinking. They are designed to provide easy-to-read and (most importantly) practical coverage of topics that are of interest to librarians and other information professionals. If you would like a full listing of current and forthcoming titles, please visit our website, www.chandospublishing.com, email wp@woodheadpublishing.com or telephone +44 (0) 1223 499140.

New authors: we are always pleased to receive ideas for new titles; if you would like to write a book for Chandos, please contact Dr Glyn Jones on gjones@chandospublishing.com or telephone +44 (0) 1993 848726.

Bulk orders: some organisations buy a number of copies of our books. If you are interested in doing this, we would be pleased to discuss a discount. Please email wp@woodheadpublishing.com or telephone +44 (0) 1223 499140.

Law Firm Librarianship

Issues, practice, and directions

JOHN AZZOLINI

CP

CHANDOS
PUBLISHING

Oxford Cambridge New Delhi

Chandos Publishing
Hexagon House
Avenue 4
Station Lane
Witney
Oxford OX28 4BN
UK
Tel: +44 (0) 1993 848726
E-mail: info@chandospublishing.com
www.chandospublishing.com
www.chandospublishingonline.com

Chandos Publishing is an imprint of Woodhead Publishing Limited

Woodhead Publishing Limited
80 High Street
Sawston, Cambridge CB22 3HJ
UK
Tel: +44 (0) 1223 499140
Fax: +44 (0) 1223 832819
www.woodheadpublishing.com

First published in 2013

ISBN: 978-1-84334-708-8 (print)
ISBN: 978-1-78063-374-9 (online)

© J. Azzolini, 2013

British Library Cataloguing-in-Publication Data.
A catalogue record for this book is available from the British Library.

Typeset by Domex e-Data Pvt. Ltd.
Printed in the UK and USA.

For Joshua and Matthew,
who changed everything

Contents

About the author

John Azzolini is a reference librarian at the New York office of one of the world's largest law firms. He is part of a professional research staff that supports the high-level, time-sensitive information needs of the firm's corporate finance, securities, insurance, litigation, and mergers and acquisitions practice groups. Prior to this he was a technical services librarian at another international law firm, Weil, Gotshal & Manges, based in New York, where he had extensive experience with cataloging and collection development.

Introduction

Abstract: Most people's images of librarianship are limited to the buildings, books, and staff of public and academic libraries. Law firm librarianship is an unfamiliar field. What do law firm librarians do? They search and manage legal information so that attorneys can competently resolve their clients' legal problems. This involves the application of librarianship's general tools and knowledge to law-related print and digital material. This straightforward definition needs to be supplemented with an awareness of the field's particular work setting. Firm librarianship is heavily influenced by the technological, organizational, economic, and occupational frameworks in which it practices. This "environmental" or interactional standpoint requires an understanding of its immediate contexts: the law firm, the law firm library itself, the legal publishing industry, and the legal research world. A timely and informative account of law firm librarianship will examine its evolving roles, tasks, and objectives as it engages with its social and material surroundings.

Key words: law firm librarianship, law firms, legal information

Imagine the following rather commonplace situation:

At a social gathering you meet someone for the first time. You are hit with that well-worn but often pointed conversational opener:

Stranger: So, what do you do for a living?

You: I'm a librarian at a law firm.

The stranger's initial response is a curious yet innocent questioning: "What is a law firm librarian? Is that like a paralegal or a legal assistant?"

You: Not quite.

Then the intrigued stranger quickly follows up with a confession: "I had no idea law firms had librarians. What does such a person do?"

Given the world's diversity of library types and legal practices, and the public's often superficial awareness of both, these mildly puzzled responses are understandable. So, why would a law firm have a librarian (or information officer) on its staff? What tasks do they perform and how do their roles serve the organization's professional objectives? *What is it that they do?*

It is time to inform all those strangers out there.

A flippant but perhaps only slightly exaggerated response to the question of what law firm librarians do is: "Anything the lawyers tell them to." A more detailed yet rather anemic answer, fit for commencing the thirty-second elevator pitch, is: "Law firm librarians use their expert searching and management skills to find legal information so that attorneys can use that information to resolve their clients' legal problems. Law firm librarianship is the application of the general tools and knowledge of librarianship to law-related print and digital material." That statement may be accurate but it does not say anything very interesting. My goal is to paint a well-rounded image of the profession. To help achieve this, I will keep a reader-respectful distance from broad, amorphous depictions as well as from the gratuitous details of work objects or processes, which are too insignificant for book treatment. I have my sights set on the fertile middle ground between generalization and granularity, borrowing from both to best convey my experiences and ideas about firm librarianship.

My aim is to present a timely, comprehensive, and practice-oriented view of law firm librarians and the professional environments that shape them. As such, this book is ideal for instructors teaching courses on law librarianship and for library school students considering various career paths and seeing law firm work as an interesting possibility. And, for anyone so interested, it can serve as a succinct introduction to the legal research experience in business-oriented firms. It is also an excellent source for practicing law librarians to revisit field fundamentals.

Every library's mission is to meet the information goals of its designated users. A firm library's users are the firm's employees. On this point, one might have the attorneys foremost in mind. As the firm's owners and primary decision makers, they qualify as its most prominent personnel. However, the library's user base also includes management and support services, which encompass such departments as business development, communications, conflicts, paralegals and legal assistants, and the secretarial staff.

The firm's collective responsibility is to serve the interests of its clients. The firm library facilitates this by satisfying the knowledge needs of the lawyers who provide direct solutions to clients' legal problems. In this regard, the nature and challenges of information access, management, and dissemination are similar across law firm libraries. The integral tasks of searching, indexing, cataloging, and organizing operate through common service, technological, and intellectual frameworks. Moreover, firm librarians as a whole are facing similar role redefinitions and expansions due to changes in these shared frameworks. Transformations in the consumption of legal information due to its online availability and the re-fashioning of law firms into business organizations are two such trends.

I will focus on these shared characteristics, keeping in mind that, since each library's operations must be aligned with its firm's overall strategy, individual libraries will perform different tasks on a day-to-day level. However, the influences of organizational size, practice group concentration, geographical region, and market location are far from controlling. Law firm librarianship is a profession best seen as united in self-conception. It possesses a fairly unified set of best practices and ethical principles. Any firm librarian will readily comprehend the industry trends and imperatives I discuss. Those not presently in the field will take away an accurate portrayal of contemporary issues and, hopefully, be better prepared when having to confront them for the first time.

Any profession is influenced by the various environments in which it transacts. There are the large-scale settings where national and global political and economic events unfold. These affect almost everyone, whether directly or through a delayed trickle-down effect. Then there are the immediate environments relating to one's occupation. The actions and decisions taken in these circumscribed settings are insignificant to vast segments of the public but to the practitioners residing in them, they are critical matters. They determine the nature and directions of the profession. Such settings are worthy of sober understanding and constant monitoring.

I have structured the bulk of this book to reflect my emphasis on this "environmental" standpoint. In the world of general librarianship, law firm librarianship is relatively small in number of practitioners and almost invisible to most people, librarians included. In the worlds of law firms and the legal publishing industry, two of its major habitats, it can seem diminutive in status and influence. Taking an interactional perspective will give one a better grasp of the varied players and forces that firm librarianship engages with, sometimes smoothly, other times discordantly. In a swiftly evolving, results-insistent field like the law, such a stance leads to a more realistic, broad-minded, and ultimately, more long-lived, footing.

Preview

The book's main chapters will examine how a particular professional, economic, or technical environment impacts the contours and controversies of firm librarianship.

Chapter 2 distinguishes firm librarianship from two types of librarians better known to the reader: public and academic. Drawing out the working conditions of firm librarians will highlight those aspects and assumptions that give their role a unique character. It will touch upon the practices of law firms that most influence the ways of the librarians who staff them. This chapter also discusses the skills and traits possessed by successful firm librarians.

Chapter 3 emphasizes the law firm as a unique manifestation of the professional service firm. It addresses the organizational and cultural frameworks that shape its practical approaches toward time, the client, and its information needs. Some of the characteristics and trends of global firms that affect the work lives of librarians are the existence of multiple offices across national boundaries, the rapidly changing regulatory environment, the rise of knowledge management, and the importance of practice groups, partnership, and revenue.

Chapter 4 looks at the characteristics of a law firm library in its role as both an information unit and a business unit. Though never entirely free of the impact of its surrounding firm culture, the firm library engages in the practices common to any business division and for-profit knowledge center. Among these are the demonstration of its value, conscientious budgeting, self-marketing efforts, managing contracts, user training, and copyright compliance.

The current nature of the legal publishing industry is the subject of chapter 5. It focuses on the market's broader competitive and consolidating directions as well as on more day-to-day themes for librarians, such as vendor relationships, pricing policies, and licensing agreements.

Chapter 6 describes how the major properties of content sources, such as their authoritativeness, exclusivity, format, and context, influence if and how a source is used. It will also touch upon the various conduits of content that firm librarians routinely exploit.

The concluding chapter will consider law firm librarianship in light of the dynamically evolving business, occupational, and technological environments that surround it. I will also venture a few predictions regarding its possible directions.

Background

A few words on my professional background...

My law firm library experience has been gained at the New York offices of two of the world's major corporate law firms. Currently, I am a reference librarian at one of these international firms. Before this position, for several years I was a technical services librarian at the American firm of Weil, Gotshal & Manges.

When I speak of law firm librarians, I am referring to reference or research librarians. Most libraries, public, academic, or private, have at least two library functions or departments, one handling technical services tasks (e.g., acquisitions, cataloging, check-in and routing of materials) and one responsible for carrying out research requests. Libraries in larger institutions such as universities may have several formal librarian positions, like those managing electronic resources, circulation, or user services. Still, the public's primary (and perhaps only) conception of "librarian" is that of the figure perched at the front desk, responding to patrons with unfulfilled information needs. Usually there is no need or interest among users – attorneys included – to consider "backstage" staff, no matter how integral they may be to the users' success at retrieving information. But I do not focus on the reference desk because of this common bias. I do so because it is my present position and therefore the one that is freshest and most pressing for my professional consideration. I was a technical services librarian for several years but reference work is my calling now. My intention is to write about what I know best.

I am aware that performing a specific job function in a particular type of organization in a certain geographical location can slant an individual's perspectives on his or her field, even if only in minimal ways. For those offering their views on matters of law, business, and society, the most fertile knowledge reservoir is often their personal experience. The key to informed and balanced writing is to keep these pre-loaded premises in sight and leverage them in pursuit of an objective treatment of the profession's shared parameters. In this regard I believe I have been faithful to my own admonition.

2

Tasks, skills, and attributes

Abstract: Law firm librarianship can be distinguished from its public and academic counterparts by examining several of the emblematic features of the firm environment it occupies: client centrality, rapid turnaround time for research results, the importance of practice groups, the prevalence of law and business resources, and the monetization of time. Success in such a setting requires certain skills and traits, such as vision, information management expertise, ability to present complex information concisely, and a comprehension of the law's diverse authority structures. To become a firm librarian means earning a graduate degree in library or information science. The job market and compensation will vary according to geographical location and firm and legal market size. Because of changing technology and business practices, law firm librarians are taking on new and demanding roles. Dynamic times are leading them to highlight their value in different ways, including the substitution of the label "information center" for "library." Enduring benefits can be obtained by joining a law librarian-based professional association.

Key words: law firm librarianship, law firms, legal information, academic law librarianship, public librarianship

Law firm librarianship distinguished from other types of librarianship

To the over-enthused library chronicler, there are countless types of libraries, as many kinds as there are kinds of knowledge-using institutions and settings. There are accounting libraries, health institute libraries, charitable foundation libraries, trade association libraries... The listing can go on indefinitely, short of one dropping from fatigue. However, such an array of fine-grained classifications, no matter how faithful it is to the mosaic of real-world library diversity, complicates the uncluttered picture of main library types held by most people. Even among librarians the categories can be sparse. There are academic (university), public, school, government, and special libraries. Government libraries are those found in parliaments, legislative assemblies, courts, and administrative bodies. Special libraries are those serving the needs of law firms, corporations, hospitals, and museums. In an even broader-stroked picture, the average person probably thinks in terms of two types, public and academic, since those institutions are most familiar through his or her local experiences or schooling days.

I will use the lay person's simplified model because its widespread comprehension gives it utility for purposes of comparison. And when addressing academic libraries, I will use the law library in its university setting as a contrasting example. As an information environment very similar in content to firm librarianship but differing in user base, time and space restraints, and organizational mission, its comparison with the firm best underscores the latter's distinctive features.

The essential goal of all libraries is to retrieve and organize information to satisfy the needs of their users. Beyond that baseline endeavor, however, there are major differences among library types regarding the nature of their users and working environments. These factors influence the way information is acquired, evaluated, and disseminated as well as how information work is perceived and carried out on a daily basis. Below are several noteworthy features of law firm librarianship that strongly affect its methods and processes. They are familiar to practitioners (who undoubtedly could point out a few that I missed). To the uninitiated, they will give a more detailed rendering of what to expect should they choose to enter the field.

Client centrality

A law firm is a professional service firm (see Chapter 2 for more on this organizational type). In such firms the successful resolution of a client's problems is the overarching goal. Indeed, this is the driving service ethic for lawyers. By dint of organizational culture, the client's centered place in the firm's worldview will also be affirmed by most of the firm's staff. If you are a firm librarian, this means the firm's client is your client. As the American Bar Association's Rules of Professional Conduct clearly state: "As advocate, a lawyer zealously asserts the client's position under the rules of the adversary system."[1] If not impelled by a corresponding zeal or adversarial mentality, the librarian must at least be motivated by pronounced levels of dedication and perseverance when tasked with a client-directed information request. When a client seeks (or demands) an answer, those at the receiving end of the question will snap into action, attorneys and librarians alike. The client's premium place in the value chain is an unquestioned fact of firm culture.

The bulk of a larger firm's clients are often commercial entities with enough resources to retain such higher-priced firms. These tend to be corporations, investment companies, business trusts, and institutional investors. Therefore, it should come as no surprise that such entities shall, for all intents and purposes, be considered the librarian's clients as well, despite the buffering presence of the lawyer who provides direct counsel. For example, a librarian may be asked to retrieve some of the supporting legal materials with which an attorney successfully advises a corporate client in acquiring another company, thereby increasing that client's market share (and the power and influence that go with it). Based on their political or ethical beliefs, some librarians might object to being placed in such a service relationship. If so, law firm librarianship is not for them. The client-based link to profit-driven business enterprises is a fundamental fact of law firms and the only way to avoid it is not to enter the field in the first place.

This all-encompassing regard for the client and the distinct workplace aura it creates are noticeably different from the public library and academic law library environments. For the public librarian, any member of the public who walks into the library with an information need is a patron, customer, or user to be served. They are almost never regarded as clients. That would imply an economic relationship that is unseemly in the public context. Similarly, university law librarians would feel at odds referring to students, faculty, or school staff as "clients." Like public librarians, they serve their users directly through personal requests or develop resources and initiatives with these users foremost in mind. The firm librarian does have direct users to serve – any firm staff member with an information want is a part of that library's user community. However, the firm client is a continual background presence and most reference transactions are motivated by the requesting attorney's duty to respond competently to a client's call for advice.

Rapid turnaround time: the norm of speed

Most law firm work occurs in the service of business interests. Such an environment is market-based, profit-seeking, transactionally complex, and fast-moving. This last characteristic needs repeating: it is a domain of accelerated interactions and rapidly unfolding events. Time is often measured in economic opportunities gained, upheld, or lost. The prompt resolution of client problems can initially be pursued for the sake of reputation enhancement, face saving, or routine corporate housekeeping, but time is ultimately about money, and usually a large sum of money. Clients oversee projects with consequential business implications. They pay sizable legal fees and expect quick, expert advice. The attorneys providing this advice will demand the same turnaround of results from the firm's support staff.

Librarians performing firm research are accustomed to this standard of timeliness. It is not uncommon to receive an urgent (and far from simple) information request that must be answered in preparation for a client call in twenty minutes. Promptness of response is also influenced by which staff member is doing the asking. In the firm hierarchy, partners occupy the top level of status and deference, and so their requests spark the most rapid response. Such an expectation of speedy results is taken for granted by firm librarians. And dispatch has to be complemented with fulfillment. Firm librarians are officially designated as salaried professionals by their human resources departments. This means there is no overtime pay for staying an hour or two past one's regular departure time to get the right answer into an attorney's impatient hands. And lunch hours are frequently as filled with searching and retrieving as working hours. The aim is a readily submitted finished work product. Professionals understand that project-free meal breaks and leaving the premises at official closing times are unpredictable bonuses.

Berring (2007) nicely illustrates the value of speed among firm librarians as compared to their counterparts in the university setting:

> When a professor asks a reference librarian in a law school to locate an obscure article, there is normally no immediate deadline staring the professor in the face. ... By contrast, when a partner in a law firm demands a piece of similarly obscure information, the law firm librarian goes on red alert. A client who is paying by the hour cannot be kept waiting, nor can a court or agency be asked to be patient. The information may be needed now. No excuses are accepted.

Both public librarians and academic law librarians strive to serve their users with resourcefulness and persistence but the sense of immediacy as found in the firm is comparatively lacking. All librarians embrace an ethic of service. High-ranking faculty members command prompt and complete attention. Members of the public who approach the reference desk are usually met with impressive diligence. However, for firm librarians this ethic is infused with an overriding sense of client exigency and consummated in an environment of demanding status-based relationships. Such a mixture establishes a norm of high-velocity information handling. Of course, this heightened speed is not an unmitigated force driving each and every task throughout one's day, but it is a parameter always hanging in the background. One should understand it as a potential that can break forth at any moment.

Billable time and matter numbers

Although alternative fee arrangements such as flat and contingency fee structuring have always existed to some extent, and seem to be gaining prominence as discussion topics among firm management observers, charging clients on an hourly basis remains the dominant arrangement.

The billing rates and other particulars of the client relationship are usually set out in a letter of engagement signed by both parties. These letters "often contain financial and other contractual terms of the relationship between the lawyer and client" (Downey, 2010). The billing formula can vary across individual clients and each client's agreement can admit several exceptions and contingencies. Such detailed coverage is beyond this book's purpose. Suffice to say, firms are paid a set rate for each hour (or increment) of work performed by lawyers on a client's matter. A matter is the industry term for a discrete project or case. The same client can have numerous matters with a single firm. Each one refers to a specific legal or business issue the firm is working on. Each matter is assigned a billing partner and a matter number. Several attorneys can work on a matter and bill their time to it.

Like other professional service firms, the law firm's business model revolves around the billable hour. Indeed, *it is* the billable hour. Attorneys are expected to bill a minimum number of hours if they want to keep their jobs. The value of individual lawyers is judged by the amount of time they bill and the percentage of this time the client ultimately pays for. These two numbers are not necessarily the same, since clients can challenge charges they deem unreasonable or unnecessary and have the matter's billing partner write them off. The more billable hours paid by the client for an attorney's work product, the more favorably the firm will look upon that attorney's prospects as a long-term asset, that is, as a potential partner. Needless to say, this aspect of firm culture heavily influences how law is practiced. Specifically, it causes an enormous emphasis to be placed on client consciousness and cost and time efficiency by all staff members.

In larger firms, many librarians bill the time they spend on research requests. Their rates are usually set out in the engagement letter. Billing for library research tends to be more common in American firms. However, anyone looking to become a law firm librarian needs to be aware of the everyday salience of matter numbers and the conditions of billable time that underlie them. It is second nature for firm librarians to ask for a matter number when taking a reference query. Even if the librarian does not bill for his or her research time, many commercial databases are designed to require the input of a matter number, in addition to user name and password, before the user can begin searching. Some firms integrate software programs into their email systems that force the sender to assign a matter number to each message.

It should be pointed out that not all matter numbers are "billable." A billable matter is one for which a particular client pays all expenses or fees generated for that matter. Each matter does, however, have a designated number. Some are simply departmental expense codes, such as for business development. Others are given to certain non-billable tasks like professional learning or article writing. But every research endeavor receives a matter number, if only for ultimate accounting, tracking, and discovery (evidential) purposes.

Billable research time would be an alien concept to academic law librarians, whose self-images are anchored to the educational missions of their parent institutions. Public librarians, who take pride in their convictions of democratic access to knowledge, would find it anathema. Both groups work for non-profit entities in information environments that are relatively free from the binding client prerogatives of the professional service firm. All libraries are now cost-conscious, budget-vigilant organizations but the firm librarian's workspace is uniquely driven by the "time is money" ethos. Similarly, the matter numbers that are basic elements of firm research transactions are absent from the work lives of public and academic librarians. The latter may have to keep close track of each completed reference task, perhaps sorting by category code and recording time spent, but this is very different from the strict matter numbering policies of law firms.

Importance of practice groups

For strategic and marketing purposes, the contemporary large law firm is composed of groups of attorneys who advise on specific areas of law. They pride themselves on being go-to professionals for resolving legal problems in their particular specializations. Although integrated within the firm's operational and administrative frameworks, these groups will be localized at the office or regional level, so a firm's Hong Kong office, for example, might be well known for handling commercial real estate transactions, while its San Francisco office will be highly experienced in intellectual property matters.

The emphasis on practice groups will affect a firm library's collection development policies, the breadth and depth of its subscribed electronic resources, and the skill sets of its research staff. Since a library builds its collection around its users' needs, a firm library's core subject resources will track closely with the information needs of its practice groups.

Some firms boast industry-prominent practice groups in bankruptcy and restructuring, mergers and acquisitions, or taxation, to name just a few. Their associated libraries will contain a large number of databases, treatises, and practice aids that revolve around these dominant practice specializations.

The collection policies and types of expertise of academic law librarians are not similarly prevailed upon by such small groups of users. A university may have an eminent faculty and sterling set of supporting resources associated with a certain subject specialization. If the law school is renowned for an area of legal scholarship (perhaps it has an institute attached to it) the library staff will undoubtedly consider the special needs of these users when implementing its collection policy. The research librarians also will be distinctly skilled in retrieving and organizing knowledge in this area. But law school libraries contain vast print holdings and subscribe to myriad electronic resources. While they may have a stronger holding in one subject over another, no single area dominates the acquisitions budget and reference time as a law firm practice group does. Since they are serving numerous students, professors, and institutional staff, academic librarians interact with a much wider expanse of legal and non-legal topics. They do not work under the sway of the practice group concept.

Public librarians research, plan, and manage with broad user groups in mind (e.g., young adults, children, seniors). Their acquisitions decisions are not influenced by anything as concentrated as practice groups. Additionally, public library systems lack the user demands and dedicated budgets to acquire the legal niche products relied on by law firms. Some of their reference librarians might field a large amount of basic legal queries from small business owners, but the knowledge skills of these librarians would lean toward breadth over depth. Most do not have the time or experience for advanced business research. A public library's user base is decidedly more diverse in its backgrounds, information scenarios, and levels of self-sufficiency than a firm library's. Such a diversity of users and user needs results in a more topically varied collection, one driven by overall usage statistics and popular demand. Its selection of titles and formats is comprehensive but can be superficial in its coverage. If a public system does contain expansive subject treatment, the relevant works may be held in different branches in various parts of a city or county. There is also the common licensing restriction requiring users to be physically present in a specific branch location to access some premium electronic databases. A firm library would be humbled when comparing mere quantity of texts with its public counterpart. However, its practice group resources and supporting reference staff serve as a single point of access for the timely resolution of critical legal issues. This immediacy and distillation of knowledge sources are the firm library's distinctive assets.

Law and business as core collections

As I noted above, most large firm clients are established businesses or financial institutions. Their operating environments are heavily regulated, litigious, and transactionally dynamic. The lawyers advising these clients must be as discerning about the structure and processes of the business world as they are about the law. And business for many commercial organizations is increasingly global. Their markets are no longer comfortably contained within national boundaries. Important developments and official rulings occur rapidly. Their ramifications are far-reaching but sometimes unclear when first occurring.

Expert counsel requires a solid comprehension of not only the long view but the big immediate picture of overlapping economic relationships and dispersed market players whose responses can be felt acutely at home. This means possessing actionable knowledge about the international interactions of law and business. Such an information need makes the firm library's business-related resources second only to its legal collection in size, currency, and authoritativeness. Customary law titles will be well supplemented by works on equity investing, stock exchanges, industry overviews, and accounting principles. Firm librarians design their collections to meet this basic need. They are also versed in delivering relevant business information to their lawyers. This can take many forms, from the routine, such as finding an overview chapter on derivatives products in a loose-leaf treatise or retrieving the historical closing prices of a publicly traded bond from the Bloomberg terminal,[2] to the challenging, such as "What steps are involved in obtaining a secured interest in a barge in Brazil?"

I state this without reservation: understanding how the business world's information sources are structured and distributed is just as important for carrying out one's job as knowing the legal domain's knowledge creators and channels.

Academic law libraries will also house conspicuous business collections and a reference staff that knows how to use them. The interrelationship of business and law is a general condition of the contemporary legal environment, so comprehending it is as consequential for the law school student as it is for the practicing attorney. A minor complicating factor may be that of established universities also having business schools with their own libraries. In this situation the law and business school libraries will have some overlapping print resources, with the latter not surprisingly possessing the larger business-related collection. While this can result in similar subject titles being kept in two physically separate buildings, the distance between libraries is usually a stroll across campus, if not just around the corner. Additionally, one-stop shopping of knowledge sources is facilitated by a copious amount of remotely accessible electronic databases, although usage of some specialty "premium" products may be restricted to those in certain programs or "schools." Some universities, for instance, limit high-end legal databases such as Westlaw to law school students and faculty. Depending on the particular institution's licensing arrangement and access rules, a similar policy may be in place regarding some business resources. But, having acknowledged these potential differences, one can still assert that business resources and their skillful navigation are as much a part of the information work of academic law librarians as they are of firm librarians.

Most public librarians do not work with sizable business collections.[3] Their acquisitions policies are implemented to satisfy a user base more heterogeneous in occupations, personal interests, and intellectual goals, so their skills will be those of generalist librarians. Some will possess specialized knowledge acquired from their university studies; others will be the resident expert on this subject or that, perhaps out of chance or individual preference. On the whole, however, the public reference desk is the reception area for any and all queries. Many of them are known-item searches satisfied by consulting readily available sources: economic or demographic data for a given date range; top ten lists; a social science review article; how-to guides on starting one's own business; a recommended biography on so-and-so. The librarian working at such a key destination point naturally acquires a broadness of information capabilities. He or she is familiar with a fuller range of general knowledge encyclopedias, popular non-fiction, directories, and indexes than the firm librarian, whose most trusted resources are smaller in topical scope yet deeper in analytical treatment.

Current, relevant law is "good law" and "on-point"

One of the pillars of competent legal representation is the proper application of "good" and "on point" law to a client's matter. In the context of legal research, a statute, regulation, or judicial opinion is "good law" if it is currently in force, that is, legally binding on those who are subject to its jurisdiction. Not having been overturned, repealed, or significantly amended, the law still stands and needs to be followed.[4] A ruling or act is "on point" if it is applicable to your specific factual or legal situation. Its scope or meaning relates to your matter at hand and you would be well advised to take account of its implications.

When receiving a finished piece of research a lawyer might explicitly ask the firm librarian, "Is it still good law?" or, "Is this on-point?" However, these are superfluous questions. The librarian always presumes the initial request carries an expectation of currently effective and relevant law. Indeed, seeking out and forwarding such resources are that librarian's *modus operandi*. Putting this caliber of material in attorney hands is the default way of doing things. A librarian retrieving older and possibly superseded legal rulings is usually one who is being asked to find archival material. Actions are affected by the laws that were in effect when those actions were committed (or omitted). An attorney might need to examine how a certain statute or regulation appeared on a past day or year, if a client engaged in something some time ago, when a different set of laws were applicable. However, in the pressing world of business law, the norm is to find presently good law. Of course, being on point is always a requirement, whether the action in question occurred yesterday or a decade ago.

Certainly, both academic law librarians and public librarians provide their patrons with current and relevant material on a daily basis. All librarians are trained in connecting information seekers with the most appropriate resources to satisfy their needs. Being up-to-date and germane are two of the most significant factors in evaluating the "rightness" of knowledge. These qualities should be sought after by anyone pursuing an information item, whether one is an experienced librarian or someone at home using an internet search engine to pull up a statistic.

With that said, I feel impelled to underscore the law firm librarian's express regard for good and on-point law. A client's livelihood depends on adeptly maneuvering through a fast moving, law-imbued environment. Professional advisers who value their reputations and repeat business must be cognizant of what law applies and how it impinges on current and future matters. Providing current on-point law to such clients is an unthinking enterprise for both lawyer and librarian. These are reflexive acts: confirming a law's currency ("Is this the most recent ruling or interpretation?"), determining the authoritativeness of the source publishing that law ("Is this the originating source, say a government agency or court, that first disseminates this type of law?"), and establishing a fit between a law's stipulations or prohibitions and the details of the matter at hand ("Does this section of the code apply to my particular set of facts?"). For the firm librarian, this line of questioning is more than a fundamental tool; it signifies fidelity to a distinct service ethic.

Getting the right information yourself and putting it directly into the requester's hands

A firm librarian's fundamental responsibility is assuring that users of the firm's information products are, first, aware of their availability and, second, utilizing them effectively. Such instructing is more than a listed job requirement, though. It is a natural inclination. Law firm librarians, like their counterparts in other settings, are instinctive teachers when the goal is getting interested users to find information on their own.

23

Considering this emphasis on lawyers effectively using the databases themselves, one might think that many firm users bypass library assistance and search the resources directly. Electronic subscriptions can be expensive, due in no small part to the premium pricing associated with licensing terms that permit firm-wide access to the product. So it is good business sense for a firm to encourage the wide usage they are paying for. Moreover, from a professional development perspective, there is much to be said for self-sufficiency on this front.

However, even with the increasing turn toward the enterprise-wide accessibility of subscribed databases and their simplified Google-inspired interfaces, firm librarians still find their search skills are consistently relied upon and esteemed. Staff members becoming expert users of online resources and rendering librarians obsolete is a non-issue. The reason for this can be distilled to a simple equation: a lawyer's time is more valuable than a librarian's. I will elaborate.

In a law firm, an attorney's billable hour is much higher than a researcher's. Clients pay handsomely for expert legal counsel from qualified lawyers. They expect informed professional advice. They also demand that the time they are paying large sums of money for is filled with a more lawyerly work product. Despite being intellectually challenging at times, legal research is considered a lesser act than analysis. Indeed, research is the data; analysis is the knowledge that makes sense of that data and facilitates decision-making. Clients are not going to pay lawyers high rates for tasks a librarian can perform at conspicuously lower rates. It is frequently in the best interests of both attorney and client to have librarians carry out the information work. The result is clients have lower costs and lawyers have time to pursue more sophisticated legal work. Even if an attorney is capable of exploiting a certain database for a desired answer, sending the request to a librarian allows his or her attention to be directed to more appropriate responsibilities, such as taking a client call or conferring with a partner in preparation for writing a legal opinion.

Time is money. It is a shopworn adage but in practice its veracity is never really doubted. When both are saved, the client places higher value on the rendered services. The client will then likely return with future business. Providing expert resolution to complex legal problems while demonstrating a commitment to conscientious billing enhances a firm's positive reputation. Such an industry-commended reputation is a mainspring of long-term success.

In a firm environment where open matters demand an attorney's quality time and clients insist on cost efficiency, the firm librarian offers prompt expertise at the right price. This is a business case for the firm librarian being the go-to person for expert information finding. As such, it leads lawyers to rely on librarians for satisfying many of their research needs. And this goes beyond applying one's seasoned hand to advanced online databases. It extends to basic searches of the open Web and publicly accessible government and company sites.

This motivating backdrop is not found in public or academic law libraries. They too have their crowded attention economies, budgetary constraints, and cost factors to contend with – but neither one is burdened by a similarly forceful weight of highly monetized time.

Patrons and students often make reference inquiries in desperation. They labor under deadlines. The right retrieved information is a necessity for completion of their projects. For multi-tasking librarians who prioritize incoming requests, the demands of senior administration and faculty members might be perceived as the university equivalents of partner queries. Receive one and you drop all the rest for the time being.

However, the work worlds of public and university librarians lack the mutually enhancing elements of billable time and client centrality. Without these, the pressure to produce cost-conscious research results with such striking immediacy is absent. Consequently, there is no compelling reason for librarians in these settings to habitually deliver a finished research product. When initiating a transaction with a firm librarian, lawyers do not have to do the information legwork themselves. When interacting with their respective reference desks, public and academic library patrons do. They are directed to relevant titles and databases and offered initial and follow-up guidance. After that, to a large extent, they are on their own. The reference librarians are available, giving support when asked, but the responsibility for directly confronting the resources and extracting answers is borne by the patrons themselves.

Skills and traits

Core competencies. Required psychological orientation. Fundamental behavioral dispositions. Many fields promulgate sets of capabilities and attitudes that are claimed to represent the necessary repertoire of a skilled practitioner.[5] They are usually published by professional bodies that have solemnly debated over the final items during numerous meetings. As such, they can possess the appearance of a committee document – lengthy, vague, and over-generalized. Delineating a formal cluster of prerequisites runs the risk of reducing a dynamic position into a series of bureaucracy-friendly check boxes on an annual employee review form. Actual practitioners who contemplate these lists tend to be deterred by their dry standalone propositions. Admittedly, the statements are intended as guidance to be aware of rather than as authoritative words to live by. But even as potential guidance in the workplace they might not rise above the status of near-invisible background markings.

There have also been journal articles and research reports exploring and advocating the skills incumbent upon information professionals to embrace or else they will wither into irrelevance. Many of these work from the presumption that we have entered a new era of knowledge creation and communication, one bringing historically unprecedented opportunities and challenges. Often referred to as Web 2.0 or Library 2.0, this environment's signature feature is a ubiquitous social media powered by 24/7 online connectivity between ideas, individuals, and institutions. This Web-centered world is said to dramatically change the nature of technology, users, and learning for practicing librarians, so much so, in fact, that it signifies the emergence of 'Librarian 2.0' (or even 3.0).[6] Partridge, Lee, and Munro (2010), for example, view this development as a "watershed." It provokes apprehension over the skills and attitudes thought necessary to survive, if not thrive. These calls to competence take a variety of forms. Librarians are gathered and interviewed, or surveys are disseminated, or content analyses are applied to past studies or to classified ads for library job openings. The results are interpreted and the ramifications are trumpeted. Or library veterans, via conference presentations, blogs, or white papers, pass judgment on librarianship's general lack of Library 2.0 preparedness and propound their own catalog of compulsory abilities and attitudes. While the labels "Library 2.0" and "Librarian 2.0" have recently been criticized as overextended and lacking in real meaning (Crawford, 2011), the technological transformations that fired up their brief popularity have become the landscape against which we all live and work.

Competencies do matter. For the sake of direction and self-insight, there is unmistakable value in publicly discussing fundamental abilities as well as debating how future skills will be defined amidst rapid change. Publishing such axioms also declares a profession's commitment to integrity, efficacy, and performance. However, core competency affirmations as set forth by associations, in quantitative studies, or by alleged gurus often have little visceral relevance to one's daily activities. Upon a closer or more sustained reading, they are sometimes betrayed to be plain common sense in bullet-point format. Some of my peers would disagree, or take umbrage at my apparent discounting of a principled undertaking, one perceived as befitting any group aspiring to professional recognition. Some association competency documents are dearly embraced by their adherents. One might even hear them cite to these documents as if they were referring to legal (or moral) authority.

However, I have never turned to these axioms for guiding influence when facing the challenges of law firm librarianship. Practitioners will acquire their capabilities and established mental approaches through years of hands-on training and experience. These competencies will vary with each individual and each work environment. Any reader interested in this field should heed the targeted words of successful practitioners. Contemplate those traits specifically relating to firm librarianship, expounded by seasoned firm librarians.[7] These will provide the most edification about what proficiencies are to be regarded and obtained.

Admittedly, my thoughts on what constitutes required competencies are personal. They are context-bound opinions but the occupational experiences that inform them are familiar to all accomplished firm librarians. Some librarians will rate things a bit differently; others will underscore a few entirely different abilities or outlooks. Interpretations of significance will vary. But all of us would attest to the insider's credibility of the others' assessments. I also admit that some of my requirements will correspond with the recommendations of associations, prominent commentators, and published studies, though expressed with a different choice of words.

I do not cleave my competency items into the usual two categories, skills and traits. Such a dichotomy is based on a convenient distinction between a person's ability to carry out a specific job or task with proficiency (a skill) and a mental or social orientation that facilitates successful performance (a trait). The former is commonly defined as the product of sustained effort and learning. It is discussed in physical or intellectual terms, something gained by long practice, study, and intention. It is an aptitude for manipulating theoretical knowledge or material objects. The skill of a medical doctor or a carpenter comes to mind. Traits are understood as emanating from one's character or socio-emotional constitution. They are cognitive or mental stances for successfully interacting with one's immediate world.

Actually, skills and traits occupy overlapping semantic ground. It all depends on where you are standing. Conventional dictionary definitions are too rigid to capture their everyday reality. What you swear is a trait may be my clear-cut example of a skill. Some individuals are born with certain skills; most acquire them through long and involved application. Traits are usually a natural part of a person's make-up, although coming into possession of one or more character strengths by way of dedicated effort and exposure is not unheard of.

There is an ineffable mix of intellectual, behavioral, and social traces in most human attributes, whether labeled "skill" or "trait." I prefer to have a simple conjoined heading, "Skills and traits," in recognition of the conceptual and practical overlay of the pair. The competencies on my list are best perceived as the finely balanced but cloaked interplay of a person's physical, intellectual, and moral capital. I believe all of them are essential to being a good law firm librarian.

Ability to analyze complex problems relating to diverse knowledge areas

All research librarians field questions on topics they have never encountered before. Such confrontations are among the reference desk's most challenging aspects. It is a source of exhilaration and learning but can be quite stressful. Though being hit with a time-sensitive request to find specific information on an unknown subject (or a small sub-section of it) is a common occurrence, it always tends to increase the adrenaline and tax one's intellectual energies. As a librarian you expect to proceed unaccompanied into foreign information territory on a daily basis, but each new request starts the process again, sending you into completely different realms.

Taking control of this process, mitigating the stress, and returning with on-point material requires exceptional knowledge seeking and recognition skills. This entails taking a sometimes sparse or incomplete explanation by the requester, who may know as little as you about the topic, analyzing its main themes, and conceptualizing these into an effective search process. Such a disposition could be perceived as a trait, since it has a lot to do with one's mental models and openness to novel situations. However, it is usually acquired via years of experience at the receiving end of indefinite and complicated queries. Like research skill in general, it is a product of long-term learning.

The skillfulness is gained by handling a multitude of reference questions, week after week. They can range from simple, known-item searches ("Get me a *pdf* copy, in US public law format, of the Bankruptcy Abuse Prevention and Consumer Protection Act of 2005") to those that free-float in the information universe, possibly answerable with available sources, but maybe only existing in the personal files of unknown experts ("Have the developed Asian capital markets experienced a decline in liquidity in the past decade, and if so, how much of one?").

Possessing an analytical and inquisitive mind is vital. The real dexterity comes from exercising that mind by continually visiting far-ranging subject matter by way of thought-sparking reference queries.

Comprehending the sources, authority structures, and relevance of law-related publications

Closely related to the analytical skill above is having a firm grasp of the scope, depth, and limitations of primary and secondary legal material. To competently handle questions with which one has a familiarity requires fluency with the structure of legal information. This intimacy is doubly important when facing completely new topics.

Being a capable researcher in any discipline stems from knowing how its authoritative knowledge is created and amended, what body or institution publishes it, and where its most current version can be found and properly cited. In law librarianship, it means knowing the rights and powers of the various law-making structures (namely, the legislatures/parliaments, courts, and administrative agencies), their jurisdictional boundaries, and the often contentious relationships they have with each other. The legal world also contemplates persuasive authority of the de facto kind. This entails a need to understand leading treatises, established practice guides, reputable journals, and the perspectives of influential players, for example, the policy positions or best practices espoused by international non-governmental organizations or prominent industry associations. These so-called secondary sources comment upon, interpret, and criticize the laws and regulations of legislators and judges in addition to providing informed outlooks for analyzing legal and economic developments.

Being aware of existing sources and deciding if their coverage and availability make them the right choice for consultation is a first and necessary step. Sufficiency is obtained by retrieving the proper resource in a cost-efficient manner. The challenge comes from navigating the plenitude of potentially on-point information. There are many knowledge creators and distributors. Frequently, there are several routes to the same document. Each one brings a different level or quality of access, pricing, and formatting. Some create primary law and make it available for free on their websites, such as governments and courts. Others aggregate primary and secondary sources in premium-priced proprietary databases. Some publish specialized subject commentaries that might include copies of relevant legislation or rulings. Others devote effort and expertise to maintaining trustworthy, open access law-related sites, such as those sponsored by universities or institutes. Some publish only in print or only electronically, others in both formats. There is the additional choice between sources considered "official," and "non-official" sources offering the same material but overshadowing the certified material with more up-to-date versions and time-saving editorial enhancements. The options are numerous and deadlines often loom uncomfortably close. An accomplished firm librarian will deliver the requested information after intuitively determining what the situation warrants in terms of cost, scope, authoritativeness, currency, and accessibility.

Information management

Most of the skills I emphasize are intimately related to each other. The successful application of one depends on the simultaneous performance of one or more of the others. Like all professional skill sets, they interact and feed into each other in hidden but significant ways. An understanding of the various frameworks for organizing and displaying information is as important to carrying out expert research as the first two skills are. These frameworks are among the librarian's most reliable finding aids: bibliographic classification schemes, structured search fields, indexes, and citators.

If the world of potentially relevant knowledge sources is strikingly large, the domain of information – that almost chaotic strata taken to be the building blocks of knowledge – can be said to be vast. This vastness is never truly tamed. As a whole, it is always expanding. Its creators and consumers interface in untold ways. The exchange of data and information is constant. What is amended or transformed (and when and how) and what stays the same (and retains its original value) are perpetual dilemmas. Of all people, librarians are keenly aware of this fact. They also know that the proliferation of knowledge is not hopelessly beyond the reach of dedicated rational efforts. It can be beneficially structured. Its scope and accessibility can be managed in the service of professional aims if one holds the proper tools of organization and retrieval.

Laying one's hands on actionable knowledge is a matter of reducing information access points to a governable number so that relevant sources can be readily found, evaluated, and utilized. This distillation process is implemented through systems both well-established in traditional librarianship and those found more commonly in law library practice.

Classification schemes and related arrangements (e.g., taxonomies, ontologies, and thesauri) have long been fixtures of all types of libraries. Law firm libraries in the United States commonly organize their physical collections according to the Library of Congress classification system (*http://www.loc.gov/catdir/cpso/lcco/*) and its subject headings (*http://id.loc.gov/authorities/subjects.html*). Firm libraries also turn to the Anglo-American Cataloguing Rules (*http://www.aacr2.org/*) for arranging how information is displayed in their online catalog records.

Evolving industry thinking on metadata creation and discovery stresses the importance of collaborative standards. Because of these concerted efforts, contemporary bibliographic control methods are sometimes drawn from heterogeneous sources.[8] This has implications for firm librarians. They must be aware of the systems used to structure their own collections, for obvious day-to-day research and collection development purposes. They must also recognize the important metadata fields found in outside institutional sources, such as large university and national library catalogs and major bibliographic utilities like WorldCat (OCLC) (*http://www.worldcat.org/*), AMICUS (Canadian National Catalogue) (*http://www.collectionscanada.gc.ca/amicus/index-e.html*), and Copac (Research Libraries UK) (*http://copac.ac.uk/*). These sources are regularly queried for knowledge-prospecting objectives and inter-library loan requests.

One need not master the rules of catalog construction like a technical services librarian. But it is valuable to know that resource discovery can be facilitated by a moderate understanding of an information item's uniformly structured metadata. One can leverage discrete parts of a bibliographic record (e.g., call numbers, title and author fields, scope notes, and subject headings) to execute a more comprehensive search for topics both frequently asked about and those never encountered before.

One of the more common methods of leveraging these bibliographic elements is the information-seeking practice known as pearl growing. This is done when a researcher needs to find material on a certain topic but is not certain which subject headings or even title words would be attached to that topic. The aim is to find one on-point resource on the topic and then extract the main headings from its catalog record for a subsequent search of any items also classified under those headings. To find subject-related books, the first few letters and digits of a known item's call number can be searched on. The underlying principle is that conceptually similar resources are assigned similar classification codes and this intellectual linking can be exploited for more thorough knowledge retrieval. Relevant books whose titles and authors are not known in advance can be discovered by focusing on this single shared characteristic.[9]

Cataloged items, in print and electronic formats, claim only a modest span of a firm librarian's information universe. Incessantly produced journal articles, industry and company reports, news stories, cases, laws, regulatory filings, and transcripts tend to dwarf the compass of standard bibliographic records. Some of this material attains findability though formal indexes and aggregated databases, but much remains scattered across websites, its retrieval dependent upon a few good terms entered into a search engine or the possession of the right URL.

Although locating internet material is often the result of sheer perseverance, librarians who rely on the Web as an essential tool in their daily work inevitably acquire search fluency. More than the average Web surfer, these reference librarians take a savvy approach toward finding publicly accessible information. They use advanced search screens and operators, quickly gauge a site's credibility, and have an evolving grasp of a topic's best internet sources. These skills, however, are not beyond the reach of many people who habitually turn to the Web for their information, news, and entertainment needs. What sets firm librarians apart is their skill at utilizing sophisticated tools to pinpoint highly relevant information. These tools are not usually found in the typical person's search kit.

Specialized indexes and high-end databases, while not exclusive to firm librarians, are essential finding aids in the pursuit of legal and business information. Each one isolates a manageable subset of resources from a much larger set, allowing the searcher to find more relevant possibilities in a time-saving manner. They parse information items into usable access points (such as author, title, publication, or topic) and allow the searcher to readily view or manipulate these points to determine if retrieval is desirable.

Most indexes that originated in print are now in electronic form, and this is the format of choice for most seekers. The wholesale migration to online platforms has blurred the functional distinction between indexes and full-text databases. Often the only real difference between them is the immediate availability of the entire digitized item in databases, although many indexes contain full-text material. An electronic database has always been able to be exploited as a type of index. Conversely, a print index loaded online can be searched and displayed as if it was a database. However, the formal definitions of either are moot when you are working intently on a project and your information-gathering tools only need to be effective, ethical, and cost-efficient.

For firm librarians (at least in the United States), Westlaw (*http://www.westlaw.com/*) and Lexis (*www.lexis.com*) are the leviathans of the research terrain, outstripping all others in scope of content, search sophistication, staff support, and marketing machinery. Due to their large size and topical diversity, these two database aggregators are sometimes referred to as integrated legal research platforms. One or the other, or both, are obligatory subscriptions for American firm librarians. I will more fully discuss them and other systems in Chapters 5 (The legal publishing world) and 6 (Research sources and systems).

The key to being an expert user of an advanced database is knowing the extent of its resources and the search language that will best retrieve what you are looking for once you determine a database might contain it. Westlaw and Lexis are illustrative of this skill's significance because they offer the most wide-ranging content and robust search options. Being aware of the options and when to advantageously use them can be challenging when confronting such complex, source-rich research platforms.

Familiarizing yourself with the ever-growing contents of Westlaw or Lexis is a daunting but necessary initial step. The most straightforward path to this end is to take time to explore their many databases by browsing their directories, which incurs no cost. Both platforms offer open Web-based directories of sources that can be searched without entering a user name and password. Spending time with these directories, visually registering their titles, and reading each database's explanatory notes go a long way towards remembering what a system has to offer. Another useful practice is to regularly read their user guides and service announcements. Both vendors consistently disseminate tip sheets, overviews, and lists of newly added sources. Subscribing to these email updates, especially those published with librarians in mind, is highly recommended.

An accomplished Westlaw or Lexis user will appreciate the significance of structured fields and Boolean operators for his or her search outcomes. Each database document, whether a review article, judicial decision, or treatise section, is divided into distinct fields, sometimes called sections. Each one is searchable alone or in combination with several others. The fields vary in number and precision with each content type, but a few prominent ones are title, author, and publication date. Combining field searching with a proficient application of query syntax (i.e., proximity operators, wildcards, truncation, parenthetical nesting, and quotation marks) allows one to delve into voluminous resources and recover on-point material in a timely manner.

Other than separately published indexes to hardcopy titles such as multi-volume treatises, legal encyclopedias, and digests, firm libraries will rarely have print indexes on their shelves. Those most instrumental for legal research are the periodical indexes. Major examples are *Current Index to Legal Periodicals*, *Index to Foreign Legal Periodicals*, *Legal Resource Index (LegalTrac)*, *Legal Journals Index*, and *Index to Canadian Legal Literature*. Many are available on Westlaw or Lexis (or the versions of these vendors licensed in a particular country) or offered as a subscription choice from among an independent aggregator's selection of databases, as offered on Hein Online (*http://home.heinonline.org/*).

In practice, however, librarians frequently bypass these formal indexes to search directly in the various full-text secondary source databases on Westlaw and Lexis. The largest of these databases can encompass practice guides, treatises, and forms books as well as journals, so the opportunity to gain such comprehensiveness is not easily resisted. But such a turn to prefabricated secondary source aggregations does not lessen the importance of indexes to legal research. Not everything can be found on Westlaw or Lexis. Some indexes, not law-related but nonetheless salient to the practice of law in an interdisciplinary society, are freely accessible on the Web or via one's local public library.

Citators are systems or tools that retrieve all mentions of an identifiable information item and gather them in a single place for convenient analysis. You turn to them when you have a case or statutory section and want to find out if any other subsequently published sources have cited your document. A cited document is usually one that has been commented upon, criticized, interpreted, or used as part of a supporting or dissenting argument. Therefore, reading those citing references is an invaluable way of learning the strength of a judicial decision's or legislative act's legal standing. Citators are prized by librarians and lawyers alike because of their ability to indicate whether a law is still "good law." That is, they collect instances of any other case or statute that threaten the status of your document by amending it, overruling it, or calling it into question. If all the citing references analyze it positively or simply mention it without assessment, it is likely still "good law".

Presentation skills

Finding the right information is an initial stage of library work. It is concluded only after that information is given clear and concise expression. How much a piece of information can stand on its own, without explanatory preface, depends on its complexity and the requester's goals. Firm librarians conduct many known-item searches in response to questions for which there is only a single right answer, for example, "What was the exchange rate on 10 February 2010 between the United States and Malaysia, as published by the U.S. Federal Reserve?" For such a query, the answer is the statistical number itself, backed by a connection to its originating source, such as an image of the data as shown on a government website.

For many other queries, the response is a gathering of supportive or elucidating material rather than a single-item answer. An attorney might ask: "How does one go about enforcing a New York State court's civil judgment in a German court?" A librarian's response to such an open-ended question can include case abstracts, review articles, encyclopedia chapters, or practice guide sections. Some of these are self-explanatory. In the absence of at least a modicum of context, others are ambiguous. Most require an introductory comment that relates the material back to the query's particulars. Since the majority of firm research requests are completed electronically, one's email message will contain a narrative set-up that informs its recipient of the relevance of the attached documents or links. Lawyers work within powerful time constraints and are bombarded with communications throughout the day. Librarians must therefore deliver their responses in appropriately straightforward language. An intelligent grasp of one's subject matter is vital. For that knowledge to be truly useful, however, the findings that come from its application need to be succinctly presented.

Digestibility and utility are paramount considerations for any format or venue in which firm librarians communicate the fruits of their research. Librarians offer group and one-on-one demonstrations of research tools and knowledge management methods. They introduce new lawyers to the library's capabilities as well as its limitations. They create pathfinders and user guides. Information can be in written form and then posted on the intranet or distributed in hard-copy welcome packs. It can involve a public lecture, complemented by PowerPoint slides or whiteboards. At the core of these communications, however, are librarians conveying easy-to-understand and easy-to-apply knowledge for the benefit of library users.

Training and teaching

Firm librarians have always been the go-to people for learning where and how to find the valuable information used by lawyers to support their decision-making. As Web-enabled products and their vendors have proliferated, so have the responsibilities of librarians for administering these systems. The library is the centralized managing hub for the firm's critical research databases and print subscriptions. A natural implication of this organizational position is making sure staff members are using them effectively and efficiently. To carry out this role, firm librarians need to be skilled trainers.

In addition to the above-mentioned presentation abilities, training aptitude requires certain social skills. Among these are an inviting demeanor that encourages interaction and comfortable questioning from one's "students"; gracious awareness of how confusing and even unintelligible a new database can appear to the novice; and sensitivity to the distinct needs and objectives of different users. A concern with constructive guidance leads to a recognition of each recipient's varying level of understanding of the presented material, how senior they are (e.g., summer associate vs. partner), and to what department they belong (e.g., litigation vs. intellectual property).

41

Service commitment

The remarkable service orientation of librarianship is perhaps its most defining feature. Serving the information needs of their patrons – it is simply what librarians do and do quite well. Working in a professional service firm only heightens the significance of this trait. In a firm setting, you are interacting with highly intelligent people who expect the same prompt and courteous responsiveness that they offer to the firm's clients. On-point research results must be delivered with an affable, polished competence if they are to serve as testimony to the library's reputation as a department of professionals. Small interpersonal acknowledgments go a long way in promoting positive regard for one's staff as a whole. Some of them might be dismissed as mere gestures. Nonetheless, they are indispensable to noteworthy customer service. Among these are maintaining assured yet easygoing eye contact, consistently using "Thank you" and "You're welcome" on the phone and in person, following up with users to make sure their problems have been resolved, and exhibiting a genuine interest in and satisfaction upon the fulfillment of patrons' needs.

Ability to work under pressure

Working in a stressful, deadline-driven environment can sometimes test a librarian's patience. One can feel overwhelmed at certain moments. Excellent customer service skills include keeping a composed exterior in the face of occupational hazards such as irate patrons and difficult questions demanding swift answers. Unquestionably, the burdens of client centrality, monetized time, and lawyerly expectations intensify the pressure. The service orientation of the general librarian must be fortified by the firm librarian's distinct professionalism. To succeed at this type of librarianship, one requires some extras – an additional layer of resilience and a slightly more advanced level of multi-tasking dexterity.

High personal standard for attaining research results

A good librarian exerts reasonable effort to find you the answer. An excellent one strives for the correct, complete, and most current answer available – and experiences self-dissatisfaction when that does not happen. As a firm librarian, I believe the successful resolution of a research problem is an internal drive. The initial query triggers a need to retrieve the best material out there. Discovering it is a personal challenge as well as a duty. Sometimes, you can find no answer despite your diligence, or you come across a smattering of published material that sort of addresses the question (but not quite). In these cases, the apparent failure to provide a gratifying response can lead to frustration and maybe a self-chastisement that lingers for the rest of the day. Firm librarians are drawn to the thrill of the information chase and know well the exhilaration that comes when securing that elusive piece of knowledge. They can also speak with conviction about the exasperation of coming up empty handed at the end of a lengthy search.

Self-confidence in one's information finding abilities

This trait is intertwined with the one directly above, since one's acceptance of high standards can only be realized if one has a sturdy belief in one's capacity to live up to those standards. Lawyers expect their librarians to be talented and intrepid researchers. They assume the knowledge found by librarians is current, exhaustive, and credible; above all, that it is actionable. Decisions relating to costly deals or legally consequential actions are initiated or supported by library research. Attorneys must be confident enough in their librarians that they do not have to second guess the material they receive. It came from the library, that suffices – it must be on-point and reputable. To uphold such a relationship, firm librarians possess an enduring faith in the vigor of their reference skills. They could not continue for long in such a demanding environment if their practical abilities were not backed by an unfading self-assurance.

Of course, there are instances when a librarian misunderstands the initial question, the requester does not express it properly, or the librarian and lawyer interpret it differently. These are commonplace occurrences in any kind of knowledge work. As such, they do not detract from the validity of my claim: a firm librarian's information handling expertise is an assumed premise held by both attorney and librarian. Even taking into account the occasional minor mistakes to which everyone is susceptible, neither party should have reason to doubt it. Interestingly, Law (2009) suggests that the librarian's reputation for expert validation can be represented as a form of kitemarking, the symbol of product quality certification granted by the British Standards Institution. Like the kitemark, the firm librarian's name and position at the bottom of the email message containing the retrieved material has the weight of a "trust marker."[9]

Adaptability to change (perhaps a fondness for it)

A skill at planning for change often appears on competency lists for all types of librarianship. Indeed, the notion of libraries in the midst of flagrant change has evolved into an unquestioned zeitgeist. The preponderant theme is one of technological transformation. The rapid rise of the Web and digital communications has created exceptional possibilities for the information professions. Libraries have been quite self-conscious of the implications these changes hold for their future relevance. This is because librarians sense the opportunities for growth by embracing the changes as acutely as they do the threat of obsolescence from *not* embracing them. Although the library literature and blogosphere are relentless chroniclers of the more dramatic scenarios of this transformation, there is no denying that changes in information access and management and in user expectations have had real and continuing effects on library practices. So it should come as no surprise that the wider industry has emphasized flexibility and innovation in the face of change as essential competencies. Some have even elevated a psychological affinity for change to a principal place on their lists.

Law firm librarians are meeting up with the same tech-based transformations. They too are contending with mushrooming amounts of information and the sprawl of vendors that collect and repackage it in various configurations and enhancements. Social media and e-books are bringing novel access and pricing issues to the foreground. Copyright issues in a digitized world are especially problematic. The legal ambiguity surrounding them is vexing for librarians who regularly interact with global peers and patrons. Immediate 24/7 availability of knowledge sources through handhelds (Blackberries, iPads, Kindles, etc) and the desktop is influencing user expectations about how directly they can search and manipulate the information they need. The specter of disintermediation sparks a questioning of relevance and identity.

Some changes are specific to the legal industry. Major publishers like Thomson Reuters and Reed Elsevier continue to buy up smaller, independent companies, prodding the advance toward consolidation and unsettling established business relationships and library practices. Law firms have wholeheartedly adopted the knowledge management paradigm as integral to the effective application of their internal know-how. Because of this development, IT-centric enterprise systems grow in stature in firm-wide knowledge strategies and new professional information roles evolve next to and possibly in competition with conventional librarianship. In the wake of the recent global economic downturn there has been a general trend in cost-cutting and streamlining. Organizational units, not least the corporate library, are being re-assessed for the value they bring to their parent companies.

At one time the customary response to the changes experienced by firm librarianship was reactive and measured, if only because the changes themselves were gradual and localized. Periodically, there were new entrants to the database marketplace, limited in number so they could fit into one's attention economy without too much commotion. And information was always increasing, although comfortably on the sidelines of occupational consciousness rather than exploding into the forefront of awareness. Industry transformations are now much wider in scale. They seem to be ceaseless, unpredictable. The library world often portrays the threats and possibilities as a bit larger and more unforgiving than non-library folks – but the changes are indisputably material. A versatile, proactive response to change is a basic survival skill. Perhaps a handier competence would be change management, which suggests a whole-body planning approach to library practice. To be successfully maintained, this anticipatory stance needs to be tempered with a naturally positive attitude. One must go beyond simply knowing how to use change; one must find it genuinely attractive and beneficent.

Vision

Vision can be a pithy inspirational word that elicits images of library leaders at conference podiums, pressing upon their audiences the need for grand thinking and grander directions. Imagining these figures speak of vision gives one the impression of collective movements putting big-theory words into field-level action (mass rallies and orchestrated chants are optional).

My rendering of the term is more modest. Vision is the individual capacity to visualize and respond effectively to the broader social and industry developments that will inevitably have a significant influence on how one engages in library work. Actually, I see it as a clarifying outlook with three distinct views. Each one provides the firm librarian with a constructive frame of reference.

One frame is leveled on what is going on in the legal world. This includes changes in the law that will influence how lawyerly counsel is given and the economic and organizational trends affecting law firm practice (such as billing/alternative fee arrangements, client expectations, staffing and cost recovery models, and profit and loss figures for firms in general).

A second frame is a recognition of relevant events occurring in the library field at large (e.g., publisher/vendor consolidation and competition, the open access debate, innovative library initiatives designed to address changing technologies and user demands, contentious issues of copyright and digital rights management, and insights into improved content delivery mechanisms and electronic resource management approaches). One does not have to giddily advocate for "big tent librarianship" to acknowledge that what transpires in public or academic libraries can often shed bright light on the ways of firm librarianship.[11]

A third frame is a comprehensive outlook on one's own firm as an integrated whole, with the library being an essential element in the firm's overall success. This means appreciating how the firm's various other departments relate to the library and what opinions they hold regarding its staff service and work quality. Most of all, it means a careful consideration of the library's perceived role in serving the firm's business and client interests.

This conception of vision is perhaps the most debatable item on my competencies list. There are plenty of firm librarians consciously armed with just one or two of the above frames who accomplish much. Some might even scoff at the notion of vision itself as fanciful or extraneous. This reaction is understandable but it might be the result of misinterpreting the word itself. Vision does not have to be a grand project. It does not need to be continuously bulging out of one's agenda or impinging on all of one's actions. It is a focused stance, a personal trait. Perhaps it is just another word for the future-oriented preparedness that fosters a more accomplished librarianship. As Sears (2006) puts it: "The professional envisions and anticipates the impact of trends on the horizon long before the 'enemy' is at the gate." Without this notion of vision, firm librarianship can become near-sighted and reactive, and such a tenuous position is vulnerable to allegations of irrelevance from those who have the power to slash, cut, and outsource.

Education and qualifications

There was a time when you could be designated a "law librarian" – in one's own eyes and in the official view of human resources – simply by working in a law library and doing law librarian "things." If you shelved, routed periodicals, copied cases, and generally helped out, you were a library assistant. But if your duties were more senior and knowledge-intensive, you were considered a librarian, with or without a library-related graduate degree.

In contemporary law firm librarianship, those days have largely disappeared. At least in the larger, urban firms with which I am most familiar, to hold the title "librarian," whether prefixed with "reference," "research," or "technical services," one now needs an advanced degree from an institution of higher learning. In the United States and Canada, the prerequisite is usually a master's degree in library or information studies, received from a graduate program accredited by the American Library Association (ALA) (*http://www.ala.org/offices/accreditation/*). Formal accreditation arrangements for library-related courses and degrees can also be found in the United Kingdom (Chartered Institute of Library and Information Professionals [CILIP]) (*http://www.cilip.org.uk/jobs-careers/qualifications/ accreditation/Pages/default.aspx*), Australia (Australian Library and Information Association [ALIA]) (*http://www. alia.org.au/education/courses/librarianship.html*), Ireland (Library Association of Ireland [LAI]) (*http://www. libraryassociation.ie/education-committee-professional- standards/recognised-qualifications/*), and New Zealand (New Zealand Library Association [LIANZA]) (*http://www. lianza.org.nz/career/qualifications*).

Extrapolating from several years' worth of reading job advertisements as well as my work-related encounters and conversations, I believe it is safe to say that anyone seeking a full-time, permanent librarian position in a large firm will need a master's degree. In the US this is usually a Master of Library Science (MLS) degree. It is a base requirement. Often, firms will ask for prior law or corporate library experience, with the average expectation being three to five years. Having past experience is not always a rigid demand. The most important skills the firm wants in a potential librarian is a good knowledge of the field's standard databases (such as Westlaw, Lexis, and CCH IntelliConnect) and the professional service orientation essential to firm relationships. These employers look for people who will be fully functioning firm librarians on their first days at the job.

Granted, exceptions are made from time to time. Some applicants are hired without solid work experience. Those who make the staffing decisions see them as highly desirable for a variety of reasons and therefore worth the extra training and accommodation. For the most part, however, there is a strong preference for hiring those with proven skill sets who can adapt to the law firm milieu rather quickly. Unfortunately, this can result in a catch-22 situation: an aspiring firm librarian with no firm experience meets resistance to getting hired but can only get that experience in the first place by being hired as a librarian with no prior experience. The problem can be aggravated by an absence of practical preparation during graduate studies. "Our graduate library science programs are simply not offering enough in the way of special library tracks aligned with employment placement opportunities ... Limited preparation is exacerbated when the client population being served has an increasingly sophisticated information literacy level so that an information professional must be prepared to add value beyond the basics almost immediately upon being employed" (Matarazzo and Pearlstein, 2011a).

It is rare for law firms to expect their potential librarians to possess a law degree. In the U.S., this would a Juris Doctor (ordinarily referred to by its initials, "JD"), earned after successfully completing three years of law school. Even among law firm directors or managers, the JD is not a necessity. This distinguishes firm librarianship from its academic counterpart. Law schools frequently advertise their librarian openings as requiring at least a JD and commonly state a preference for job candidates holding both an MLS and a JD. Butterfield (2007) explores the varying expectations, practices, and attitudes pertaining to different types of law librarians holding a JD degree.

Job market and compensation

There is no single source of reliable and all-inclusive data on hiring and salaries of law firm librarians. Employment markets and compensation structures vary according to several factors. Country, geographical region, city, and firm size and prestige are some of the more determinative ones. Another parameter, perhaps not one considered until recently, is the extent of firm layoffs and hiring freezes attributable to the economic crisis of 2008 and subsequent downturns. This too could vary by legal services market and result in diminished hiring prospects for support staff such as librarians.

An additional barrier to attaining a comprehensive portrait of the firm librarian market is the fact that law firms, as privately held organizations, do not readily divulge the salary details of their personnel. Therefore, it is difficult to arrive at even general estimates.

In the US, the most reliable survey of law librarian compensation is the AALL Biennial Salary Survey and Organizational Characteristics published by the American

Association of Law Libraries. Since it "reaches the broadest segment of law librarians and has the highest response rate of other comparable law library-related surveys," (Cadmus and Orndoff, 2009), it is the most reputable and relied-upon. The most current version is the 2011 edition. Conducted by an independent research firm, it runs to over 200 pages and analyzes the responses of 3337 individuals on multiple categories, including organization type, geographical location, years of experience, and education. Impressive for its thoroughness, data quality, and visual presentation, the Survey can rightfully claim that it is "the only source of comprehensive, comparative salary information for law librarians who work in academic libraries, private law firm and corporate libraries, and governmental law libraries." (Ibid.)

Although the Survey combines private firm and corporation libraries, one can still get a useful sense of the compensation scheme for firm librarians in major American geographic regions. For example, the mean annual salary of a reference/research librarian in a private firm/corporation in New York City is $82,983 (the median is $82,650). For the same librarian in Boston, it is $67,283 (median: $67,000). San Francisco and Chicago both have a mean of $76-77,000 (median: $78-79,000). It is not surprising that the highest salaries are offered in the largest metropolitan areas, where the legal markets are most active. For instance, the Washington DC metro area, with a mean of over $76,000 (median: $73,212), is among the most populous of urban areas, but it can also offer highly competitive salaries because, as a global center of political power, it contains the offices of many prestigious and profitable national and international firms.

The British and Irish Association of Law Librarians (BIALL) publishes an annual Salary Survey. At the time of this writing, the latest is 2010/2011. It contains the responses of 147 members, analyzed by organization type, level of responsibility, duties forming a significant part of one's job, and attitudes to work. To give one an idea of compensation among law librarians in London, the United Kingdom's largest city and dominant legal market: the law firm median salary for a full-time Librarian/Information Officer in London City is £29,700. For the rest of the UK it is £23,100.

Salary surveys, even the most professionally prepared, analyzed, and presented, are imperfect indicators of a field's compensation structure. They are susceptible to the natural weaknesses of the method. Its manifest drawbacks are a lack of representativeness, low response rates, and the application of standardized questions that return simplified responses but fail to capture a complex reality. Considering these limitations, aspiring firm librarians should use surveys only as a supplemental tool to assist them in deciding whether to enter the profession.

New roles

Firm librarians are inevitably affected by the technological and market changes impressing upon their parent organizations. They are also experiencing the role transformations that librarianship in general is undergoing. Especially notable are those resulting from widespread digitization of information in all its forms and the growth of media channels to access that information.

Role changes can vary in dramatic timbre. For some librarians, the same basic work responsibilities and expectations remain as much a part of the job as ever, but in different or enlarged forms. This is usually seen as "business as usual" albeit with some expanded ground to cover. For others, however, there are completely new tasks and positions, not previously assigned to the library, but now often added to its work load because of departmental reductions or consolidation or because the library has been recognized as a source of cost-effective expertise. These changes come with a more graphic countenance. They arouse more consternation because they introduce different sets of obligations, sometimes competing with the ones already attended to. These transformations are often hoisted onto librarians, suddenly and compulsorily, so they also provoke more resistance.

Both kinds of changes are stressful in raising the standards of what constitutes a worthy firm librarian. In other words, these new roles are now defining features of what management expects in firm librarians if they are to be appraised as value-producing assets. The stakes are high because, as Will (2008) states: "These days the library is much more part of revenue generation."

Among the more gradual changes are heavier involvement in reviewing and negotiating vendor contracts, more dedicated efforts toward marketing the library as a results-driven unit, and a need for library managers and directors, if not librarians, to become comfortable and capable with traditional business tools such as budgetary projections and financial statement analysis. These augmented roles are partially due to technological progression: librarians are recognized as being the most skilled users of large-tag electronic subscriptions, so they have been put in charge of keeping tabs on those contractual terms that best serve (or dis-serve) the firm's interests. Additionally, these essential legal products have become accepted items of library budgets. Once this placement occurs, the close relationship between the library and the information product is assumed to be the natural order of things. Administering the licensing aspects is merely an expression of that order.

The augmentation can also be traced to the evolution of the legal services market and perhaps of business practices in general. Confronting an increasingly competitive environment and recent economic downturns, firms have adopted the same cost-cutting ideology as their corporate counterparts. They have streamlined operations and applied stricter value standards to remaining departments. Staff responsibilities have increased. As Egan (2008) has pointed out, among library managers this has led to "a new round of professional development needs that involve mastering metrics, developing productivity measures, reviewing budgets as line items as well as reviewing budgets in terms of firm initiatives, presenting, negotiating contracts, and identifying staffing needs."

An instinctive response to the demand for departmental justification is self-promotion. Many firm librarians are now very active marketers for their internal "brands." They feel a constant need to prove their value to attorneys and management, if only to distance themselves from the stigmatic label of "cost center." Work product is affixed with a prominent library logo. Outreach attempts multiply in order to raise one's profile for the regard of decision makers. Some have even shed the title "Library" and taken on new names, ones that are believed to better reflect a firm-aligned strategic nature (see section below: labels and name variations).

A more unsettling role transformation is effected by firm librarians being forced to shoulder wholly new job functions (such as conflicts or dockets management) due to departmental consolidation. Librarians' skills and capabilities are often rated highly enough that the administration sees delegation as a logical step. But even if the restructuring stops short of consolidation, there may be an official partnering of the library with other information-dependent units like business development, competitive intelligence, and knowledge management. These associations, even if unofficial, lead to more inter-departmental claims on the library's resources. Management's expectations will correspondingly increase and remain at that elevated level. In some cases, the library is combined with these other units on an equal footing that is not adequately clarified. Lines of authority and professional priorities can become ambiguous. Tensions and job dissatisfaction may grow. In an extreme scenario, the library might be subsumed under the aegis of another department, such as information technology.

Those entering the field should be aware that librarians, particularly in larger firms, are experiencing considerable role modifications, some of which are inherently stressful. Many of the transitions are variously interpreted, depending upon individual experience and temperament. Some librarians will feel anxiety where others sense an exhilarating challenge. Others may readily adapt without much concern one way or the other. But whatever the personal response, one must anticipate dealing with a definite undercurrent of change in the profession.

Labels and name variations

A periodic though not very pressing issue in law firm librarianship is the perceived need to re-name (or re-brand) the library. For some firm librarians, the word "library" is assumed to carry semantic baggage, if not palpably negative connotations, for managers reviewing departmental budgets. Such librarians believe that administrators see the term "library" on their ledgers and are overtaken with imagery of obsolete books, periodically re-shelved and re-arranged by equally obsolete 'librarians," with both print and people taking up valuable firm real estate. "The library" is allegedly a thing of the past. But re-titled "The Information Center," for instance, and the library is transformed in management's eyes. Same staff, same tasks and expertise, but now it reveals itself as truly in the service of the firm's knowledge goals. With this new name supposedly comes a new, more favorable estimation from the powers that be.

Every now and then, one hears of a firm library taking on a new name. As far as I know, nobody is keeping track of how many have made the change. Reading library blogs, listservs, and industry literature, I have come across it a few times. Taking a look at the 2011-2012 membership directory of the Law Library Association of Greater New York (LLAGNY), a chapter of AALL covering New York City and including many of the world's largest firms, I can see a handful that designate themselves with names that do not include the word "library." One calls itself an "Information Resource Center" and its staff members are "information specialists." In the directory's 2007-2008 edition, this firm uses the titles "library" and "research librarians," respectively. It is probably safe to assume that not long ago most of these "resource centers" called themselves "libraries." I am sure each of these eminent firms established itself in the legal market while in proud possession of a "library."

Of course, LLAGNY members tend to be among the biggest firms and there might be a more noticeable trend to re-name among mid-sized firms. However, I am not aware of any widespread move in that direction. The push for an alternative label is a rather recent phenomenon. It remains to be seen whether more firm libraries will designate themselves with new titles or if such re-branding is a limited and passing trend.

Recently, one of the more newsworthy and controversial re-naming events in librarianship was the Special Libraries Association's (SLA) 2009 proposal to change its name to the

Association for Strategic Knowledge Professionals (ASKPro). The proposal was one element (though apparently a large one) in the SLA's Alignment Project, an extended and well-funded research and marketing initiative "to help define a position for SLA as well as the profession" by setting "a strategic course to ensure that the significant value of librarians and information professionals is effectively communicated and understood" (Rink, 2009).[12]

The Association took note of the sweeping technological and market transformations affecting its members. It believed there was a profound disconnect between what information professionals affirmed as their valuable contributions and what so-called C-level executives (the CFOs, CEOs, and CIOs who call the budget and hiring shots) wanted the information center or library to be contributing if it was to be judged as value-adding. SLA hired outside communications and analytics firms. Presentations and supportive articles were disseminated. As Bates (2009) pointed out, the goal was to convince the decision-makers of the "connection between our information sources and their strategic decisions."

The name proposal became a contentious issue of discussion on blogs, listservs, and Facebook pages. Strong opinions were entrenched on either side. The measure was soundly defeated in December 2009, with 2071 in favor and 3225 against. Turnout was impressive, with about half of all eligible members voting. There was much speculation on the reasons behind the rejection. An informative selection of these was compiled by Greg Lambert from comments of the Texas Chapter of SLA. Among the reasons were a poor choice of alternative name (especially its acronym, ASKPro); the SLA leadership's poor handling of the process; and a belief held by many members that they were not allowed enough input. Oder (2009) also provides a good overview of the voting outcome.

Although the name change was perceived to be the Alignment Project's culmination, the thinking behind the initiative has given the notion of strategic value an invigorating push into the membership's consciousness. The strong debating was fertile ground for a critical re-examination of issues of professional identity, adaptability, and organizational responsiveness. If anything, the heartfelt and reasoned responses to the proposal gave special librarians a heightened appreciation of how they were perceived by their parent organizations – and what they must do to remain a valued part of them.

In my experience, I have yet to come across imputed deficiencies in the library that could be addressed by re-christening it with a new and improved title. I have never been privy to upper-level management meetings where departmental fates are determined, but I find it difficult to believe that, at least at the firms I have worked, the word "library" spontaneously invokes images of obsolescent print-pushers whose most commanding skill is depleting the firm's resources. And if administrators did make this assumption, no name change or re-branding crusade could do much to prevent its inescapable finale. Most managers, indeed, most lawyers, do not have time to contemplate the overtones of the term "library." "The library" is where that needed-right-this-moment answer can be found. "The library" is where partners send associates to get a crucial informational foothold for comprehending a client's complex legal issues. "The library" contains the people who facilitate access to all those vital online subscriptions, the significance of which is realized only when that access becomes problematic.

I do not have an inordinate emotional investment in the title "librarian." I am sure my work attitudes and professional self-image would not change much if I suddenly took on the title of "information specialist," although this vague and somewhat pretentious designation might pique more curiosity from casual acquaintances than "law firm librarian." Conversely, I feel no unease or insecurity when being called a "librarian." Perhaps this is the insider in me speaking. I know fully what librarians are capable of. I do not require full-blown marketing engagements to recognize their ongoing ingenuity and qualifications. The "librarian" label is far from a negative one for me.

It is also doubtful that attorneys would hold this negativity. After all, they each spend several years in a law school environment where the law library is still a "library" and a valuable if not indispensable conduit for learning. Despite facing changes similar to other library types, the law school library is still an esteemed place in legal education, for its skilled and responsive staff as much as for its symbolism. So I cannot imagine firm lawyers being too eager to jettison the "library" as if it represented excess baggage. If there is an intimation of obsolescence, it may come from those attorneys in managing positions who have been out of law school for a long time. Their positive memories of the library might have faded, made indistinct by too many years of not having to perform much hands-on research. Of course, if these senior lawyers do harbor unfavorable impressions, adopting a new, flashier brand will not stop them from striking you from the budget. An unnecessary expense, whether it is classified as a "library" or an "information center," is something that has to go.

Associations

Professional associations are venerable, enduring, and perpetually metamorphosing. New ones are always sprouting. Established ones adapt, innovate, merge into newer, larger versions, or wither and fade away. But the constancy of the form is a given. And so is its utility. Associations are among the most functional of social groupings. They are here to stay.

In a Web-centered era, the professional association and librarianship make for an ideal reciprocity. Librarians are expert stewards of distributed digital information. They are infused with an unparalleled service ethic and possess genuine respect for sharing among themselves (as well as with the public). Web 2.0 is also highly distributed, user-focused, and intensely collaborative. The right tools and attitudes are in place for librarians and their associations to flourish together. For law firm librarians no less than for public or academic librarians, the annual fee for joining an industry association is nominal compared to the copious benefits received.

There are countless testimonials to the highly positive aspects of association participation.[13] For the many practitioners who have been members for a while, even a short listing of these benefits is a preaching to the choir. They already know what they are getting. However, for those not yet involved, some of the rewards are touched upon below.

Knowledge sharing

Members acquire useful professional knowledge, new practice tips, and updates on fast-breaking industry developments through discussions on the associations' well-maintained and active listservs (distribution lists).

Professional development, networking, and employment opportunities

The association website and sponsored luncheons and training events offer opportunities to learn about the latest job openings, initiate rewarding personal and professional relationships, and keep one's skill sets up-to-date.

Enhancement of a sense of community

Continuing interaction with mutually supportive peers under a shared banner creates a stronger professional identity and, presumably, reinforces one's sense of purpose and pride in one's work.

Lobbying efforts to serve members' interests

Librarians can often be as politicized as they are collaborative. Associations are focal points of lobbying endeavors to influence local, regional, and national legislation on matters related to information policy, privacy, and copyright. They are also formidable advocates for libraries against the intemperate price increases and questionable commercial methods of powerful vendors.

Blogs, wikis, journals, and presentations

In addition to listservs, associations disseminate important insights and current awareness via the blogs and wikis of their various chapters and special interest sections. They also publish journals and magazines that include more substantive theoretical and empirical investigations. Members often send out links to transcripts, presentations, and podcasts of industry speakers from seminars and symposia spotlighting a diversity of library topics.

Annual conferences

The larger library associations hold carefully planned and widely publicized annual meetings where hundreds or thousands of members socialize, network, exchange ideas, connect with vendors to offer feedback or grievances, try out new products, and attend myriad training and educational sessions. As Breslin (2012) puts it, "Nothing beats meeting and interacting with other people from within your profession, people who face the same problems as you do, and people who might well have an answer to those problems."

Law library associations vary in size and reach. Usually, the influence of an association is felt most strongly in its home country. A Web-encircled world is very likely increasing the international communication and visibility among formerly localized associations. Some of the more established and active associations are below.

American Association of Law Libraries (AALL)
http://www.aallnet.org

Australian Law Librarians' Association (ALLA)
http://www.alla.asn.au/

British and Irish Association of Law Librarians (BIALL)
http://www.biall.org.uk/

Canadian Association of Law Libraries (CALL)
http://www.callacbd.ca/en/content/home

International Association of Law Libraries (IALL)
http://www.iall.org/

New Zealand Law Librarians' Association (NZLLA)
http://www.nzlla.org.nz/

Organisation of South African Law Libraries (OSALL)
http://www.osall.org.za/

Scottish Law Librarians Group (SLLG)
http://sllg.org.uk/

Special Libraries Association (SLA)[14]
http://www.sla.org/

Of particular interest to law firm librarians are the following association divisions/sections:

SLA Legal Division
http://legal.sla.org/

Private Law Libraries (Special Interest Section of the American Association of Law Libraries)
http://www.aallnet.org/sis/pllsis/

Notes

1. American Bar Association. Model Rules of Professional Conduct: Preamble & Scope. Online at: *http://www.american bar.org/groups/professional_responsibility/publications/ model_rules_of_professional_conduct/model_rules_of_ professional_conduct_table_of_contents.html*.
   The American Bar Association (ABA) is a voluntary professional association of lawyers. It "provides law school accreditation, continuing legal education, information about the law, programs to assist lawyers and judges in their work, and initiatives to improve the legal system for the public" (*http://www. americanbar.org/utility/about_the_aba.html*). Its Model Rules are ethical standards and guidelines, lacking the force of law. However, as the ABA is the largest and most influential attorney advocacy group in the US, the Rules have an inordinate power to sway industry practice. In addition, the Rules have been adopted in whole or in part by 49 of the 50 U.S. states. When adopted by a state legislature or court, they are legally binding.
2. Bloomberg Professional (*http://www.bloomberg.com/ professional/*) is a proprietary database offering current and historical equity, debt, currency, and commodities pricing

information, real-time financial reporting, in-depth company and market news coverage, and primary and secondary legal sources. Often referred to as the Bloomberg Terminal, it is visually distinguished by twin monitors, a multi-colored keyboard, and a data-intensive interface that is manipulated by entering a vast array of combined three and four digit commands. Far from intuitive, Bloomberg is intimidating to learn and its search logic can be confounding to even experienced Westlaw and Lexis users. However, its data sets and analytical functions are invaluable to sophisticated business research.

3.   This is not an absolute statement. Some large metropolitan public library systems have branches designed specifically as business libraries. The New York Public Library's Science, Industry, and Business Library (*http://www.nypl.org/locations/ tid/65/about*) is one such example. Having been established with these communities of practice in mind, it contains exceptional business-related collections as well as a research staff adept at managing and searching them. Note: At the time of this writing, the Library has published a controversial plan that calls for, among other projects, the sale of this Science, Industry, and Business Library. See Pogrebin, (2012).
Other examples of public institutions with excellent targeted resources are the City Business Library of the City of London Libraries (*http://www.cityoflondon.gov.uk/corporation/LGNL_ Services/Leisure_and_culture/Libraries/City_of_London_ libraries/cbl.htm*) and the British Library's Business and IP Centre (*http://www.bl.uk/bipc/*).

4.   A law or ruling can be heavily criticized on legal grounds by courts in nearby jurisdictions (such as adjacent states or districts). This does not prevent it from being good law, since these other courts lack precedential power outside of their jurisdictions. However, they sometimes wield a persuasive authority that might make lawyers approach the questioned law more cautiously.

5.   For those competency lists most relevant to law librarianship, see:
Private Law Libraries (PLL), Special Interest Section of the American Association of Law Libraries: Core Competencies for Head Law Librarian.

(*www.aallnet.org/sis/pllsis/Toolkit/ToolkitCoreCompetencies.
pdf*)
American Association of Law Libraries (AALL): Competencies
of Law Librarianship, revised April 2010.
*http://www.aallnet.org/main-menu/Leadership-Governance/
policies/PublicPolicies/competencies.html*
Special Libraries Association (SLA): Competencies for
Information Professionals of the 21st Century, revised June
2003.
*http://www.sla.org/content/learn/members/competencies/
index.cfm*
Also, PLL publishes a similarly motivated "Commonly Asked
Questions and Answers about the Value and Work of Law
Librarians."
http://www.aallnet.org/sis/pllsis/Toolkit/ToolkitQA.pdf

6. For discussion of the importance and ambiguities attached to
"Library 2.0" skills, see Abram (2007), Holmberg, Huvila,
Kronqvist-Berg, and Widen-Wulff (2009), Nonthacumjane
(2011), Saint-Onge (2009), Saw and Todd (2007), and
Partridge, Lee, and Munro (2010).

7. For a very brief overview, see Durrant (2006). For a fine
anthology addressing the abilities and outlooks needed by
contemporary firm librarians, pick up Aspatore's *The Changing
Role of Law Firm Librarianship* (2008). Other valuable
publications for discovering what firm librarians actually do
are "Day in the Life" style articles, which tend to be informal
and often humorous. See LeDoux and Bohls (2007),
Abramovitz (2007), Devlin (2007), and Coolidge (2007).

8. Taylor and Joudrey (2008) survey the numerous metadata
frameworks of the library and archive communities, making
plain their reciprocal influences and important convergences.

9. For an excellent overview and great insights into library
research methods, information organization, and the proven
tools of accomplished librarians, see Thomas Mann's two
books: *Library Research Models: A Guide to Classification,
Cataloging, and Computers* (1993) and *The Oxford Guide to
Library Research*, 3rd ed. (2005).

10. Although Law's piece was written in the context of
university libraries, his reference to a confirmed reputation

for searching-and-filtering expertise is expandable to all kinds of librarians. The Good Housekeeping Seal can be seen as the American equivalent to the United Kingdom's kitemark. However, over the years the phrase "Good housekeeping seal of approval" has often been used facetiously in popular culture, so it might not have the same gravity as the UK mark.

The Kitemark:

http://www.bsigroup.com/en/ProductServices/About-Kitemark/

Good Housekeeping Seal

http://www.goodhousekeeping.com/product-reviews/history/welcome-gh-seal

11. For a skeptical and provocative stance on the idea of "big tent" librarianship (that is, the notion that all librarians, no matter the type, have a deep-seated connection to each other), see "Public Library Privilege," the March 16, 2011 posting of the Library Journal's Annoyed Librarian blog. Online at: *http://blog.libraryjournal.com/annoyedlibrarian/2011/03/16/public-library-privilege/*.

12. For background material, presentations, and articles, go to the Alignment Project page at: *http://www.sla.org/content/SLA/alignment/index.cfm* and the Alignment Portal at: *http://www.sla.org/content/SLA/alignment/portal/index.html*.

13. See Bird (2012) and Kirk (2012) for a few good introductions to the joys of library associations.

14. The Special Libraries Association (SLA) embraces members from all types of so-called special libraries (e.g. business, medical, museum, law firm). However, its value to law firm librarians for educational, networking, and advocacy purposes is undeniable. It also offers a Legal Division geared specifically toward the interests of firm librarians.

3

The law firm

Abstract: Of the several professional environments affecting
the practice of law firm librarianship, the structure and culture
of the firm itself exerts the strongest influence. The law firm
shares the general characteristics of professional service firms
but these features are given distinct expression when found
among organized legal practitioners. Lawyers' unique views on
client service and the monetary value of time and their constant
interaction with large amounts of dynamic information
determine the library's attitudes toward knowledge, collection
development, and customer service. This influence is especially
compelling for librarians in global firms. A library's local
office is dominant in its everyday projects but being part of a
partnership of multinational offices with interfacing practice
groups will have a bearing on how library work is carried out.
One's perspectives on the legal information industry's leading
issues are impacted by one's location in such a resource-rich,
big-deal-oriented firm. Other significant environmental factors
are the ever-changing legal and regulatory developments in
greater society to which law firms must respond, the specter
of librarian displacement by the recent rise of outsourcing,
and the general turn to knowledge management systems to
administer the vast quantities of information generated by
large companies.

Key words: law firms, law firm librarianship, professional
service firms, partnership, legal knowledge, knowledge
management, outsourcing, intranets

The structure and culture of the law firm itself are the most immediate influences on the firm library. The large firms this book centers on are usually formed as partnerships.[1] This decisive identity bears heavily on the firm's methods and attitudes regarding work product, compensation, status, and career development. But perhaps more significant for the impact it has on its library is the fact that the law firm is a professional service firm in the business of providing expert legal advice. Becoming familiar with the ways of this distinct business entity will clarify how firms and their libraries approach issues of knowledge, service, and the client relationship. It is essential for understanding the most direct and pressing of the environmental factors that affect firm library operations.

The law firm as a professional service firm

"Professional Service Firm" (PSF) is a descriptive label applied to organizational forms that share certain features. Widely accepted definitions are difficult to come by, but Empson (2000) offers this broad one: It is "any firm that uses the specialist technical knowledge of its personnel to create customised solutions to clients." A large law firm is almost always a professional service firm, especially if it has branches in more than one national market. However, a PSF is not always a law firm. It can be an advertising, accounting, or consulting firm.[2]

For law librarians working at large firms, the importance lays in the implications the following service firm characteristics have for library practices: knowledge-centeredness; the client relationship, the billable hour and monetized time; and the notion of leverage.

A *knowledge-centered environment*

Law firms are knowledge-intensive organizations. They apply expert knowledge to facilitate legal and commercial transactions and resolve the problems that arise from such transactions. Although the considerable efforts expended on knowledge management systems attest to the trans-situational relevance of certain forms of knowledge, the intellectual work brought to bear on a client's matter is mostly customized. That is, the lawyer's analysis, fact-finding, and counsel are tailored to address the distinct needs of the client's current situation. Each new matter involves a different combination of facts, applicable law, immediate and third parties, and financial or personal ramifications. The legal advice given is the result of carefully considering the interplay of these variables.

Large numbers of clients translate into a diversity of factual, legal, and analytical parameters to keep track of. Multiple cases are worked on simultaneously. The details of each matter must be individually assessed. Progress must be regularly checked and reported to the client. Such complex information-processing responsibilities can create significant cognitive challenges for attorneys.

This information plethora will also affect firm librarians, though not with the same levels of inundation and exigency. The enormous amounts of knowledge stemming from a firm's many matters come in both actual and potential forms. On the one hand, there are the known and recorded particulars to attend to: established data and facts; applicable laws already applied; and secondary sources already consulted. On the other hand, there are the developments and turns of events that may occur at any time, forcing a wider cast of the knowledge net. Information types and topics not contemplated yesterday may become must-have knowledge sources later today or sometime tomorrow.

For example, a client may approach a law firm with the following situations.

The client ("Company A") is a prominent publicly-owned American telecommunications company in talks to acquire and merge with an equally large public US Telecom ("Company B"). The firm is retained to advise on the possible antitrust (anti-competitive) implications of the merger. The legal counsel is excellent; the merger is given the go-ahead by the US authorities. However, after the agreement is completed, the merged company becomes the target of a major governmental investigation, which was sparked by questionable practices allegedly performed by Company B before the merger. Negative publicity is widespread, the financial interests of the merged company are threatened, and a criminal prosecution is pending. The client (now the merged company) is taken to court by its minority shareholders for breach of fiduciary duty. The litigating shareholders claim Company A's directors should have been aware of the events that lead to the investigation, if not the probability of the investigation itself. Legally obligated to protect shareholder interests by a duty of care, the directors would not (or should not) have gone through with the merger. That is the lawsuit's contention. The client returns to the firm, seeking further excellent counsel.

A large team of lawyers and business services staff will work on these matters, as their facts and legal issues are numerous and complex. Some attorneys would delve into every possible point of law and acquaint themselves with all the relevant details. Others might concentrate on one or two points, depending on how involved they are with these particular matters or on what point in the timeline they entered.

As support personnel with less client involvement, the firm librarians would be less intimate with the matter's full range of variables. A librarian might be asked for answers on a specific legal aspect and not be informed of the other issues at play. One librarian might research point of "law A" while another might answer a query relating to point of "law B." Often, librarians are given a few pieces of the puzzle without knowing there are other pieces. Indeed, several of those absent pieces would make for an enlightening pattern if placed side-by-side.

However, regardless of having a sparseness of research-ready leads, a librarian always works with the contingency of needing to know how to perform reference work for all applicable points of law, A to Z. This requires versatility for discovering and exploiting any information resource relevant to the matter at hand. Seeing the overall picture and its interrelated components is often pivotal for both expert legal advice and expert research. One must be capable of assessing the authority structures of unknown knowledge areas, and do it under strict time restraints.

Despite coming from the same client, the two matters above would probably be handled as two distinct research threads. Each of the threads might have several topically interconnected sub-threads. The librarians who field queries on these matters would be called upon to provide different kinds of information. Frequently, the differences have to do with legal subject, type or level of research, and source.

1) <u>Legal subject</u>: Law is defined by its jurisdictional limits, both subject and territorial.[3] In the US, an antitrust matter is a federal consideration; corporation law is found in each state's statutes. There are also judicial, statutory, and regulatory domains, federal and state. Each enforces rules or laws and adjudicates in matters they are authorized by their constitutions or legislatures to preside over.

For the first situation the legal team will need to know the established body of law and formal and informal practices of the federal regulatory agencies empowered to oversee antitrust issues. Antitrust laws are codified in the United States Code (*http://www.gpo.gov/fdsys/browse/collectionUScode.action? collectionCode=USCODE*) and interpreted and applied by federal district and appeals courts (*http://www.uscourts.gov/ Home.aspx*). They are enforced by two administrative agencies, the Federal Trade Commission (FTC) (*http://www. ftc.gov/bc/about.shtm*) and the Department of Justice (DOJ) (*http://www.justice.gov/atr/about/index.html*). The FTC's regulations are contained in the Code of Federal Regulations (*http://www.gpo.gov/fdsys/browse/collectionCfr.action?collec tionCode=CFR*), which is updated regularly via newly adopted or amending rules published by the agencies in the Federal Register (*http://www.gpo.gov/fdsys/browse/collection.action? collectionCode=FR*). Federal agencies also publish manuals, policy statements, and frequently-asked-questions (FAQs) on their websites for the education of the public and those companies whose industries come under agency jurisdiction.

Since the merging companies are public (their shares can be bought and owned by anyone, from institutional investors to everyday working people), some of their activities are closely regulated by another federal agency, the Securities and Exchange Commission (SEC) (*http://sec.gov/*). The SEC's oversight actions are many and complex. They stem from its chief obligation to protect the investing public, which includes both current stockholders and potential investors. This responsibility centers on ensuring the capital markets operate in a fair and orderly manner and overseeing the ways in which company information is publicly disclosed. In service to these goals, the SEC enforces rules relating to the prompt and transparent communication of a company's existing financial condition and forward-looking estimates, its entry into material contracts, the legal proceedings it is party to, and any changes to its board of directors, controlling stockholders, or insider ownership. This agency's official regulations are also updated in the Federal Register and then codified in the Code of Federal Regulations. Additionally, its website contains an abundance of primary legal sources, guidance, and educational material for casual investors, researchers, investment advisers, and accountants.

Since the companies are publicly traded, they must abide by the listing rules of the stock exchanges they are traded on. In the US, the New York Stock Exchange (NYSE), the American Stock Exchange (Amex), and NASDAQ are prominent exchanges. Each has requirements pertaining to corporate governance, stock price, and shareholders that must be initially met and then maintained. The applicability of these rules and their interpretations by the exchanges themselves and the federal courts must be considered in the total mix of binding authorities.

A big challenge for lawyers and librarians is sorting out the legal interrelationships and ranking order of the various judicial, legislative, and regulatory authorities that come into play. One needs to know what ruling bodies, decisions, and interpretations claim priority in what particular situations and in what measure. It is crucial to be able to discern the authority structure of the jurisdiction that holds sway over the factual situation you are working with. Experienced firm librarians will gain fluency with such authority structures, although the perpetually changing and sometimes convoluted nature of law-making means one should never take anything for granted. Always consult the originating legal sources and their reputable commentators.

Primary sources such as statutes and case decisions can be very general or very fact-specific. Sometimes a lawyer requires explication from respected secondary sources. For such clarity, librarians are likely to recommend standard treatises, law review articles, or law firm memos on corporate mergers and their antitrust or anti-competitive aspects. One go-to source for topics in antitrust situations is Areeda and Hovenkamp's *Antitrust Law: An Analysis of Antitrust Principles and Their Application.*

For the second situation, involving fiduciary duty, let us assume the company is incorporated in the state of Delaware. This jurisdiction is the most common choice of incorporation for large American public entities. Delaware also has the most established body of corporation case law, as decided in the closely watched Delaware Court of Chancery (*http:// courts.delaware.gov/chancery/*).

The research team would turn to the estimable Delaware corporation law treatises, *The Delaware Law of Corporations & Business Organizations* by Balotti and Finkelstein and *Folk on the Delaware General Corporation Law.* These invaluable sources provide straightforward explanations of the statutory provisions on establishing and maintaining a Delaware corporation as well as analyses of the prevailing case law that have interpreted the statutes. Both are available in print or electronically via the CCH IntelliConnect research platform (*http://www.wolterskluwerlb.com/ intelliconnect/*), where they can be easily browsed or meticulously searched.

For the second situation, librarians will also be fielding several questions on securities law issues. The laws applicable to a public company's actions and disclosures are not always clear and comprehensible to an attorney new to the field; the regulations implemented to flesh out these statutes can be doubly unintelligible. Adding to the interpretive sprawl are the many SEC-published persuasive sources, such as no-action letters, compliance and disclosure interpretations, and staff legal and accounting bulletins.

Some are legally binding, others are not, but all are undeniably guiding for securities advisers. In such a substantive area of law, finding an established treatise or practitioner guide (in print or online) is a common move, both as an initial step to become familiar with the basic issues and as part of one's ongoing research needs to obtain a more nuanced understanding.

The secondary resources dedicated to securities practice are impressively large. They range from single-volume primers to multi-volume loose-leaf treatises. Some are succinct summaries of the major securities laws. Others are highly detailed treatments of specific topics, such as the legal remedies for fraud or the regulation of investment advisers. Some are in print only, some have print and electronic versions, and some are only online.

Many practice areas consistently turn to one or a few treatises for expert guidance and proven theoretical insights. These texts are considered industry standards. They are staple items on firm library shelves or among its electronic subscriptions and are often cited in judicial opinions and scholarly articles. For corporate finance practitioners, *Securities Regulation* by Loss, Seligman and Paredes is such a standard. It offers authoritative analysis of the many legal issues arising from securities-related business developments, case law, statutes, and administrative decisions. In print, it is a comprehensive eleven volumes long. It is also accessible online through the CCH IntelliConnect platform. Because of its deep and dependable coverage of securities fundamentals, *Securities Regulation* is a reflexive first choice for firm librarians seeking to get a definitive handle on the controlling law in this area.

2) <u>Research type or level</u>: The level of research sought depends on several factors, the most prominent being the

information objective, skill set, and background of the requester. The query might be for a known item, that is, something the requester knows actually exists and has some bibliographic information on. This could be a law review article with a known title or a case decision where the parties and year are given. It might be a request for introductory material on a broad topic, such as the major congressional acts that created the antitrust regime in the United States. Or it could be an open-ended research question, for example, has the Delaware Court of Chancery decided any cases involving an alleged breach of director fiduciary duty shortly after a merger completion and, if so, are there any secondary sources offering analysis of the issues? A less experienced associate could ask for a subject-specific general introduction, whether in the form of a handbook, nutshell, or single-volume condensed treatise. A veteran practitioner might want a simple refresher on a handful of procedural points. For that query a few select chapters of an industry-standard practice guide might suffice.

3) <u>Source</u>: In addition to an abundance of content, a firm librarian's knowledge environment is rich in sources, providers, and formats. Increasingly, resources originating in hard copy are being loaded as online versions, the same electronic publications are being offered by several vendors, and voluminous information items are being posted to the Web, competing for attention with the unbounded data and documents already there. This creates an extra cognitive challenge for librarians. Added to the plethora of information topics is an array of methods for delivering that information.

Of course, not all formats or sources are created equal. The research situation you face will often influence which sources are more equal than others, at least provisionally. Some are designed better, with superior content and overall functionality. Some are preferable for certain requests because they are more cost-efficient to download or simply free. When choosing one source or format over another, an experienced librarian factors in several variables, often unconsciously. These include the complexity of the request, any time or cost constraints for providing the research, the availability and perceived credibility of the material, and the requester's need or desire for a distinct format.

For example, if an associate wanted grounding in a company director's fiduciary duties under Delaware law, you would refer him to the sections on this subject as covered in Balotti and Finkelstein's *Delaware Law of Corporations & Business Organizations*. There may be one copy of this treatise on the library shelf. It might be on loan or the lawyer may be seeking a word-searchable version of the book, for which a print volume would be unaccommodating. Since your firm has a firm-wide subscription to the CCH IntelliConnect research platform (which contains the online version of the Balotti book in addition to several other outstanding corporation and securities titles), you can direct the associate to the relevant sections via an emailed hyperlink, or you can download the sections into a single pdf and forward them.

A senior partner delving into more granular issues of fiduciary duty might be looking for something more focused or expansive than text sections from Balotti and Finkelstein. An industry standard on this specialized subject is Stephen Radin's *The Business Judgment Rule: Fiduciary Duties of Corporate Directors*.

In fact, assume the partner explicitly requested this title. Firm libraries with active corporation law or mergers and acquisitions practices would likely have this book in hard copy. It is also accessible electronically through CCH

IntelliConnect. But what if you did not have this title in your collection? And what if you did not subscribe to this particular resource on CCH, since it is cost-prohibitive for your firm to maintain online subscriptions to every available IntelliConnect resource? Thankfully, the request is not an urgent one, but it still needs to be fulfilled in a reasonable amount of time. Another alternative is to try and borrow it via inter-library loan from a local firm (since many universities will not loan books to for-profit organizations).

This, however, presents other obstacles. The current edition of the Radin book is a hefty four volumes, running over 6000 pages long. Some firms are reluctant to loan such large items. Also, as a topical go-to source, this publication might not be lent out to other firms. Since it is frequently consulted, it needs to be kept in-house for the research requirements of one's own staff. Yet another option is to ask the requester if he knows what topics or specific sections he is interested in. If he does indeed know, you can submit a request to a library listserv, hoping some list recipients have the book in their collections, it is available on their shelves, and they are willing to photocopy, scan, and email the relevant pages. If the requested number of pages is too many, most librarians will balk at the request, and you are out of luck. If you cannot get your hands on a borrowed set or on photocopied pages, you may have to purchase the title for your collection, or add the electronic version to your IntelliConnect subscription (providing you already have such a subscription). The request might not be so urgent that you need to provide the information within minutes, but it will likely be required soon. This means buying the print copy and having it shipped by the fastest method of express delivery possible or obtaining prompt approval to add the *Business Judgment Rule* module to your existing online account and getting the vendor to activate immediate access.

A librarian might be asked to retrieve certain anti-competitive statutory and regulatory sections, say certain sections of the Hart-Scott-Rodino Antitrust Improvements Act of 1976 and the regulations promulgated under that act. The request may be for the primary law itself, without editorial enhancements, or it could be for the law plus any clarifying annotations, for example, case citations from specific jurisdictions or law review treatment from the last ten years. The bare-bones statutes can be accessed for free via the Federal Trade Commission website (*http://www.ftc. gov/bc/hsr/hsrbook.shtm*), where the link for the Hart-Scott-Rodino Act brings one to Cornell University Law School's Legal Information Institute, a highly reputable site for open access primary legal material. The administrative regulations for the Act can be found at no cost at the website of the US Government Printing Office (USGPO) (*http://www.gpo.gov/ fdsys/browse/collectionCfr.action?collectionCode=CFR*), which publishes the official edition of the Code of Federal Regulations. For value-added enhancements, one has to turn to a sophisticated online citator, either KeyCite (on Westlaw) or Shepard's (on Lexis). A cost is incurred for their use but they are unique tools offering a large and customizable selection of citing references for U.S. case decisions, laws, and regulations.

As one can see, successfully navigating the legal information world's many sources and formats is a matter of nimble choice management. Free or fee? Print or electronic? One's own collection or inter-library loan, or perhaps a document delivery service? Premium database for advanced functionality and visually appealing format (and premium pricing)? Or the unadorned primary law itself from a government website, no-cost and direct from the official source but lacking in user-friendly formatting and printing options? Or perhaps a legal subject is covered in a subscribed database, one already paid for by an annual flat fee, boasting IP-authenticated firm-wide access and unlimited searching and downloading, but offering much less search sophistication and content coverage than a high-end, pay-as-you-go resource like Westlaw or Lexis. Researchers will evaluate the particulars of the situation: the user, the legal topic, time and cost parameters, source feasibility. They will make an informed judgment call.

I created the above antitrust and shareholder litigation situations to illustrate the information handling and organizing challenges confronting law firms. It is a bit simplified, using broad legal areas, but it is not so far-fetched in the world of large corporate firms. I wanted to underscore how information in such an environment is unceasing and potentially limitless. There is increasing attention to the relevance of non-law resources to legal practice. The sources for legal and non-legal information are expanding to more free websites and offered for a price by a growing number of commercial vendors. The immediate communication of new developments creates an expectation of 24-hour connectedness and real-time responsiveness. The options are many and the time frame to make the choices is usually narrow. Appreciating this aspect of one's work terrain is one mark of the professional law firm librarian.

The client relationship

As a professional service firm, a law firm holds its clients in very high regard. Indeed, the perpetuation of gratified clients is its reason for being. However, it is more than a mere provider of expertise in exchange for financial remuneration. The law firm privileges the client relationship more intensely than, say, the advertising or consulting firm because the stakes involved in the practice of law are much higher than those facing other service firms. Lawyers advise on billion-dollar deals where financial ruin is a possibility for both sides. A failed business transaction – and sometimes even a successful one – can threaten the livelihoods of hundreds of its participants, direct (investors and owners) and indirect (company employees) alike. As importantly, law firms counsel clients in the ways of carrying out profitable enterprises without incurring legal risk or challenge. And if the courts are already involved in a client's situation at the time of a firm's engagement, lawyerly advice is relied upon to mitigate or avoid civil or criminal sanctions. The firm manages a client's most consequential risks: the punitive remedies of the legal system and the heavy monetary losses of corporate deal-making. As Castanias (2011), the Library Partner at global firm Jones Day, plainly asserts: "Our clients put their businesses, their jobs, and sometimes even their lives in our hands; if we are doing our jobs right, they belong to us."

Recognizing the client's high-stakes nexus helps one to better understand the firm's particular organization and ideology. A group of dedicated individuals, similarly educated and trained, self-regulated by the bar and adhering to its code of professional conduct, join together in a partnership of peers to practice law, a complex and very serious line of work. Its ethical culture is devoutly embraced. Its intellectual objectives are pursued with vigor. This is a formula with a proven track record. The firm's exceptional standards of diligence, advocacy, and commitment are perfectly tailored to promote a consistent level of client service in a contingent, big-risk world.

This prioritization of the client suffuses all levels of the firm. I introduced this principle of client centrality in Chapter 2. Librarians are as beholden to the ethic as the attorneys. When responding to reference requests, a librarian is aware that the client is not far behind.[4] The attorney may be doing the direct asking, but the librarian's response, whether in raw form or partly informing an analysis, will be for the benefit of a client matter.

In fact, the notion of the client relationship is more of a general service template that librarians work from. They implicitly apply it to most of their dealings with other staff members. The conception of the client transcends the actual client, which is the business entity hiring the firm for legal assistance. In their daily activities, firm librarians apply expertise towards the resolution of their clients' information problems. Attorneys, paralegals, secretaries, and business development managers are all clients in this underlying sense.

Firm librarians cannot help but be influenced by this perspective because it is a basic tenet of the firm environment. Those not accepting it and remaining faithful to it will find themselves seeking employment elsewhere. But it is mistaken to assume that this creed of the client is grudgingly accepted or somehow resented as a contrivance. Its adoption is part of a beneficent socialization. The typical firm librarian readily embraces it as a professional obligation. He or she perceives it as a motivating goal, something to take pride in when it is carried out with finesse.

Client dedication is one of the pillars in the firm's goal of protecting legal and economic interests against material risks. That is its institutional function. At the individual level, consummate client service fosters an invigorating bond between the service provider and the client. As Smets et al (2009-2010) assert, service

> encompasses a process of implementation and a strong sense of social engagement...The ability to engage with clients at an intellectual and social level can enhance information exchange, reduce tensions and make

eventual crises appear more manageable. The 'feel' of the transaction is often considered as distinctive a service feature as the quality of the product and the efficiency of its delivery process.

That is, an accomplished client relationship can be emotionally and socially gratifying for the parties. For the provider, it spurs an ambition to succeed, backed by perseverance and tenacious efforts. It impels you to be at the top of your game, whether you are a lawyer giving advice or a librarian performing research.

Billable hours and monetized time

The main source of revenue for professional service firms is the money billed on an hourly basis by staff members working on client matters. In law firms, most of this billing is done by attorneys. Billable rates are based on seniority or experience. Partners have the highest rates, beginning associates much lower, and paralegals and librarians lower still (although not all firms bill for their librarians' research time).

The attorney-client relationship is a professional bond. It is strong with considerations of loyalty and trusteeship (in the broadest sense of the term), but it also contains a forceful pecuniary element. Bills for legal work can be quite high, due to the cost of expert counseling and administration and the numerous hours and staff members devoted to the resolution of a complex matter. With more hours worked, firms generate more revenue. More billable hours also means clients incur higher legal costs. Consequently, both lawyers and clients have an acute consciousness of the monetary implications of engaging a firm for high-level problem-solving.

Aside from the substantial and sometimes contentious issue of billing arrangements, both lawyer and client work in an environment where financial risk is a naturally large part of the landscape, especially for the latter. For the players involved in major deal-making, the possibility of heavy gains and losses is always in the room, at times obvious but unspoken, like the proverbial elephant, though frequently sprawled across the table and incessantly attended to. The world of international business and its legal counsel is grounded on the pursuit of capital. And both the perils and the rewards can be prodigious.

In such a setting, time becomes thoroughly monetized. Firms expect their attorneys to work a minimum number of billable hours if they are to remain in good standing. To many lawyers, the designated minimum can seem an unreasonable expectation that must nevertheless be accepted if they wish to continue as large firm lawyers. In addition to being exceedingly stressful, it can lead to one perceiving his or her personal and professional time in largely economic terms. Hours worked and hours wasted are reflexively translated into dollars gained and lost. The pressure is intensified by the client's demands for a high quality work product that often necessitates many hours of intellectual application. Frequently, conclusive answers are demanded for difficult questions under merciless time constraints. And all the while there is that overbearing risk-infused canvas of expensive deal making and breaking.

Although they usually do not interact directly with clients, librarians are well socialized into the firm's comprehension of the client relationship and the corollary of monetized time. They are affected by this world-view because its legitimacy and emotional tenor are readily transmitted by the attorneys who turn to the library for answers. The marked value of both an attorney's and a client's time is also underscored in the alacrity with which research queries are expected to be carried out. I referred to this in Chapter 2 as the norm of speed.

The preponderance of the client and a collective recognition that its matters are legally and financially consequential compel an extraordinary level of responsiveness in firm librarians. Indeed, as commented on earlier, librarians believe in a diffuse notion of the client and the service ethic it inspires. It encompasses the disembodied business client represented only by a matter code as well as the firm attorney visiting the reference desk with a standalone question. Some conception of the client imbues each request. This fact is one of the biggest influences on the way firm librarians approach the daily practice of librarianship. It results in the library adopting the earnest professionalism of its parent institution. It leads to a business-oriented librarian who sometimes applies an immoderately commercial sense of time, cost, and efficiency to information work. This may be seen negatively, depending on your grasp of what a librarian should be doing, but in the law firm environment, it is an unquestioned asset.

This cognizance of monetized time explains the firm librarian's habit of fielding not only those difficult questions for which seasoned researchers are uniquely qualified to handle, but also straightforward queries that lawyers can seemingly answer for themselves. I will mention this situation briefly, since I described it in the last chapter, under the heading, "Getting the right information yourself and putting it directly into the requester's hands."

When a client hires a professional service firm to resolve its problem, it pays a premium price for expert advice. This know-how is expected to come from the firm's deemed experts. In a law firm, these are the associates and partners, those staff members with enough training and experience to offer effective counsel. Attorneys render the opinions and propose the lines of action that expedite or preclude front-page organizational actions. The client is only concerned with this final product. As such, the time of those providing this product is considered to be of much higher value, reflected in their hourly billing rates and a near-universal acknowledgment of their high occupational status.

Librarians provide the authoritative information that confirms and corroborates – but they are and will always remain administrative staff. Their responsibility is to serve the fee earners who are serving the clients. In such a supportive capacity their time is worth comparatively less. From a librarian's perspective Lambert (2012a) fittingly sums it up: "We do certain pieces of the overall work for the client and firm so that the attorneys can focus on practicing law and bringing the best value to their clients." For example, in terms of personal capability, a lawyer may be able to access a commercial database to retrieve a publicly filed company agreement, but at the same time he needs to prepare for a client conference call as well as a one-on-one meeting with his supervising partner. Lambert again: "Just because a lawyer *can* do certain parts of the work, does that mean that the lawyer *should* be doing that part of the work?" The answer is an emphatic "no." A quick call or email to the library is far more time-and-cost-efficient.

The practice of firm librarians retrieving the requested information themselves can be attributed to more than simply the relative value of an employee's time. Harvey (2003) sees this active approach as a signifier of true professionalism. He distinguishes between a "facilitator" and a "signposter." "The facilitator will find the answer to the question on the enquirer's behalf; the signposter will merely point the way referring the enquirer to sources where the answer may be found." Sometimes a requester needs to do the basic research himself, such as when an informed analysis is immediately required and the library staff is unavailable (unlike lawyers, librarians are not on call 24/7 – *yet*). Harvey mentions the case of trainees, who often should do the legwork themselves to become familiar with standard sources and methods. However, most firm librarians, most of the time, are full-fledged facilitators.

The global firm

The size and geographical expanse of a law firm will affect the operations of its library (or libraries). Information work in an international firm[5] is influenced by how legal knowledge in such a coordinated enterprise is produced and shared. At the same time, though, a firm library's research and collection development practices are heavily shaped by the staff needs of its local office.

Multinational offices and locality

By definition, a global firm has offices in several countries. The largest firms boast a presence in twenty or more nations, where they are fully staffed by domestic and expatriate lawyers and business support personnel. As of this writing, the law firm of Baker & McKenzie, for example, has 71 offices in 44 countries and employs over 4000 qualified lawyers.[6]

A global firm works on matters adjudicated by multiple legal systems. These can involve a standard business transaction in a single jurisdiction or a sophisticated undertaking in several interacting ones, as in cross-border mergers and acquisitions. In this latter type of matter, international firms are key players in a world of increasingly globalized law. They "sanctify the relationships that global actors form when they engage in business. Without the imprimatur granted in the documentation of the large law firm, business dealings will always appear somewhat profane and suspect." (Flood, 2007)

As highly competitive, well-integrated organizations, international firms create and maintain extensive bodies of know-how related to numerous domestic and foreign regulatory regimes, market conditions, and deal practices. This knowledge is contained in the firm's precedent and document management systems but it is applied by experienced practitioners alone and in collaborative teams. Deep and broad legal understanding is quickly communicated between practice groups in different regions.

The international law firm epitomizes the knowledge-thriving professional service organization. The librarians staffing such a firm have access to a plethora of legal, business, and industry information. Much of it will relate to foreign jurisdictions or unfamiliar practice areas. Some of it will be internally produced, accessible though the intranet; some will be found in external sources, in the continually growing files of subscribed databases. While not expected to be proficient researchers in the laws of numerous countries, by virtue of their positions as point people for information in general, librarians are expected to at least be able to identify the individuals in the firm who could perform such research (or who can point the inquirer in the right direction). For example, the librarian in the Bangkok office can likely obtain a copy of those new Stock Exchange of Thailand arbitration rules if the Washington DC staff is having trouble finding them. Or, a London information officer is the best source for retrieving the most current aircraft leasing agreement template governed by UK law. Conversely, the Moscow attorney who seeks a quick introduction to how

New York State courts interpret mutual termination in contract cases would be wise to shoot an email query to the New York library.

Being a vital knowledge hub in such a dynamic global organization can be a truly fulfilling experience. Many librarians are pleasantly challenged if not invigorated by the abundance of information, the multinational interactions, and the diversity of research topics. Moreover, the prospect of participating in sophisticated, heavyweight deals, even if only indirectly and from the sidelines, can make large firm librarianship an exciting occupation.

However, a firm library, despite being one among several office libraries spread across two or three continents, will handle mostly queries and resources related to its home office practice groups as well as to the general practice of law. This latter domain of law itself has a strong jurisdictional component, since legal actions and prescriptions normally take place in a certain geographical location and are thereby subject to its jurisprudence. Therefore, a library's print collection, its subscribed databases, and the typical reference question will usually relate to the actual laws (and interpretive secondary sources) of the legal system governing its local office and to the law pertinent to that office's practice areas. Though a practice group often has firm-wide staff and projects, librarians tend to field questions from the team members in their local offices.

There is a minor exception to the above-mentioned propensity toward localized information work. In international commerce (with which large firms are inextricably linked), the choice of law provisions in binding agreements refer to English or New York law more often than not. These are the contractual clauses that establish the forum for resolving legal disputes. As Flood (2007) asserts, these two jurisdictions are the only ones with the "appropriate rules and norms" for conducting financial services transactions on a global scale. "Most transnational agreements will at some stage be transcribed into one or both of these systems." The firm librarians who regularly work with deal lawyers are not expected to have expert knowledge of both sets of "rules and norms," but they will become familiar with the significance of these two jurisdictions. And, when tasked with a question regarding English or New York law that is beyond their compass of knowledge, they can always turn to their peers in the London or New York office library (assuming their firms have offices in these locations).

Importance of practice groups

The practice of law, reflecting the trends and transformations of larger society, has become too complex for generalists. The economic landscape is marked by continual cross-border exchange, technological innovation, and the actions of regulatory bodies both governmental (the traditional nation-states) and intergovernmental (e.g., the United Nations or the International Centre for Settlement of Investment Disputes). It is a complicated and volatile era for practitioners. Globalizing trends in capital investment, communications, and information creation and delivery have imparted existing legal areas with interpretive ambiguity.

Overlapping areas of law are emerging from this interactional mix. Such domains can be procedurally and substantively unsettled. The business enterprises that enter them often require specialized counsel in multiple practice areas, so they place their matters in the hands of large commercial law firms, the proven one-stop legal shops for a rapidly globalizing world. To meet this demand, large firms offer departments of experts focused on particular legal areas, such as taxation, shipping, or real estate. These highly experienced groups coordinate international offices and project teams to effectively manage the challenges of modern commercial transactions, which often encompass numerous legal issues in addition to several parties and their distinct jurisdictions. Smets (2008) proposes that "the relevant issue for clients when seeking to engage a professional adviser is not so much the firm's general reputation, which the client may not care much or may not be able to make a judgment about, but that of the focal practice."

I introduced the significance of practice groups in the second chapter. To briefly reemphasize: their biggest influence on the library will be on its collection development policy, its budget allocations for subject-related print and electronic subscriptions, and the research strengths of its staff.

The size of a practice group will have content and administrative implications for a library through its influence on determining what material should be purchased, updated, and cancelled. A prominent group may have substantial practice resources at its disposal via the library shelves or databases maintained by the library. The continuation of these subscriptions and the start of any new ones often rely on the approval of practice group heads. The cost of these niche products can be quite high. They will likely be billed to the groups that requested them or use them most. But even if they are not taken out of the library's own budget, the periodic accounting and usage monitoring for such resources will be the library's responsibility.

However, the absence of overt guidance from practice departments is no excuse for librarians to overlook the subject-specific dimensions of their collections. They are expected to take a proactive, functional, and cost-effective approach to acquisitions. A vital collection enables lawyers to advise on their field's fundamental matters as well as its emerging issues, enduring controversies, and current developments.

All firm librarians are assumed to possess a fundamental proficiency in searching and organizing diverse information sources. They are also expected to know the general authorities and publication channels peculiar to law librarianship. I addressed several of these competencies in the previous chapter. Successful firm librarians show real dexterity in navigating the structure and processes of legal information.

But, despite a shared foundation in universal reference skills, there will be differences between firm librarians in their specialized knowledge bases. These distinctions are frequently attributable to the information requirements of the practice groups they support. Some librarians will be adept at patent research which, to an outsider, might seem an intimidating sphere of high-priced databases, esoteric search terms, and overly technical literature. Some have know-how in retrieving the convoluted language of tax statutes and regulations and the extensive primary and secondary source guidance that follows their publication.

My firm's New York office, where my library is located, contains a prominent corporate finance/capital markets practice group. We have a solid selection of online and print sources that meet the research needs of this team. A librarian gains subject expertise when taking all levels of reference queries and consistently turning to these resources. One of the strengths I have gained is a confident grasp of the multi-faceted legal structure of the US securities decision-making bodies. Another is a power searcher's resourcefulness in finding particular disclosure language in public company filings to the Securities and Exchange Commission (SEC). In a regulatory system based on precedent authority, this identification of disclosure language accepted by the SEC in previous filings is a daily necessity for corporate finance attorneys.

Partnership and leverage

Most large firms are organized as partnerships. This is a form of business association in which equity interests and decision-making are concentrated in the hands of a limited number of owners, referred to as partners. A lawyer is usually offered partnership (or "made partner") when firm management determines he or she can bring the firm substantial revenue through client development, thereby advancing the firm's monetary interests and reputation.

A firm partnership has distinct characteristics that by themselves will not have much influence on the practice of firm librarianship, but which librarians still need to be aware of and sensitive to, since they affect their workplaces' culture regarding staff interactions and relationships.

One of these aspects is the status hierarchy of the large law firm. Lawyers in general will occupy a manifestly higher position of status than the support staff – the paralegals, secretaries, finance and billing analysts, information technology people, etc – sometimes simply referred to as "non-lawyers." Attorneys are the firm's viable intellectual capital, the fee earners who meet, manage, and satisfy the clients. Partners, though, as the firm's major stakeholders and administrators, stand at the hierarchy's top.

Even if unspoken, most staff members – lawyers and non-lawyers – are aware of these status differentials, and would admit to their existence without hesitation if asked. Much staff action is related to client service, even if only tangentially, but attorney work has a more immediate and material connection to the actual clients. And, after all, they are the ones logging almost all of the billable hours. For librarians, as with everyone else, this means there will be customary differences in wait times and project prioritization. That is, lawyerly needs are fulfilled before those of human resources or communications or ... the library.

Of course, any complex organization is a site of many buffers and intermediating players. Differences in treatment can be mitigated by a request initiated by a lawyer but delegated to a succession of staffers. The information query emailed from a trainee solicitor appears a bit less compelling than one sent by a senior counsel. But, since requests often are made on behalf of attorneys and therefore are just as important as if they were submitted without an intermediary, the same levels of responsiveness and service (should) apply.

Needless to say, social interaction being what it is, direct personal contact will always have a more pressing, behaviorally stimulating quality. A receptionist phoning the library with an inquiry from a partner is an action-inducing call. That same partner walking up to the reference desk with the inquiry has just galvanized a more acute reaction – of responsiveness and perhaps of anxiety.

Another prominent characteristic of large law firms is the notion of leverage. Empson (1999) describes it through a lens of professional development: "Junior staff work alongside more experienced staff in close-knit project teams and learn the trade through an informal apprenticeship process."

Leverage, however, is also a dependable business model, says Harner (2011):

> Law firms employ several nonequity lawyers for each equity partner. Law firms then compensate equity partners in part through revenue generated by the billable hours of nonequity lawyers (who are paid on a fixed salary basis). Essentially, law firm profits are generated through nonequity lawyers' billable hours.

Leverage itself does not influence how firm librarianship is practiced. But it makes good sense to be aware of the concept's significance as a method of generating revenue and as a basic way of structuring interaction between junior and senior staff members. Associates work on several different projects simultaneously. These include client-billable matters and non-billable jobs such as contributing to presentation material or compiling a background file for a pro bono case. Often, numerous associates are assigned tasks for the same client matter. Supervised by a partner, they will bill their time to the one matter. This is how younger attorneys gain legal and industry experience, the firm earns money, and clients receive well-orchestrated and timely counsel.

When the term "leverage" is used, it customarily refers to lawyers, namely, the ratio of associates to partner. However, in a general (and contestable) sense, it could mean a leveraging of non-equity lawyers *and* support staff such as paralegals and librarians for the effective and cost-efficient resolution of a client problem. In this interpretation, an optimal mix of lawyers and business services people are consciously assigned to a particular matter, taking into special consideration each member's background, skills, and billable rate. Arguably, a looser version of this blend is already used in the average large firm, since a variety of departments contribute their efforts to any matter that calls for their assistance. Some bill their time; many do not.[7] However, a more explicitly weighted arrangement of complementary competencies and rates could make for a more efficient client approach.

Presently, the partnership structure of most global firms seems entrenched, as a method for distributing profits, a form of professional socialization, and an ordering of status relationships. For those entering law, the idea of partnership is robustly appealing. This captivation goes beyond the incentive of monetary reward. There is a vitalizing collegiality, an identification with larger, collective goals, and a burgeoning of professional self-regard. Empson (2006) points out the rousing social quality: "Typically, in those firms with a strong partnership ethos, it represents a powerful unifying force among the partners which serves to counteract the self-serving impulses that drive each partner individually." Riskin (2012) accentuates the thrust to one's occupational trajectory when he states that "It's not just ego, it's really positioning – it affects the way this individual will be perceived professionally." Again, these are organizational realities that firm librarians should be cognizant of, if only because it is a wise strategy to know the contours and forces of one's work culture.

Partnership, though still a viable business model, has been facing challenging developments. For global firms especially, the opening of overseas offices and an expansion into international markets have forced firms to adopt management structures similar to those of "managed professional businesses," if not of multinational corporations (Segal-Horn and Dean, 2007). Key decision-making and even strategic management are increasingly in the hands of non-lawyers (Hitt, Bierman and Collins, 2007). The integration and maintenance of such a large operation by the partners themselves is inconceivable. The result has been a delegation of daily administration to finance, human resources, communications, and facilities managers.

In light of the substantial amounts of personnel and dollars involved, a more hierarchical "corporate" scheme of planning and supervision can be irresistibly cost-efficient. Large firms employ thousands of people and generate hundreds of millions of dollars in revenue. According to the 2012 Am Law 100 survey (*http://www.americanlawyer.com/PubArticleTAL.jsp?id=1202549382505*), the industry's most watched ranking of law firm finances, the top seventeen US firms had over one billion dollars in gross annual revenue (The American Lawyer, May 2012). The top four had over two billion. In the same publication's ranking of the world's firms, the Global 100 (published every October), the top twenty-one on the list had over $1 billion in revenue in 2010 for their most recent fiscal year (*http://www.americanlawyer. com/PubArticleTAL.jsp?id=1202514393371*). With these numbers, the practice of law might be perceived as just another case of taking care of business.

Another challenge to the idea of partnership as a calling above that of simple commercial enterprise is the way the Web-enabled legal press and independent media outlets such as blogs have opened up the workings of firms to constant scrutiny and criticism. "These new media emphatically presented law as a business and lawyering as a competitive career in which the players were in large measure responsive to the financial incentives of the market" (Galanter and Roberts, 2008). This sometimes too-close-for-comfort coverage of the profession's mergers, rankings, departures, and controversies has had the effect of attenuating its traditional claim to being nobler than a mere for-profit industry.

If you are a support staff member such as a librarian, this can give you the impression that you are working in simply another sweeping corporate business, albeit one whose chief product is expert legal advice. And, given the size, capital, and complexity involved, the feeling is not entirely unjustified.

One possible effect of working in such a dominant international firm is that it will instill in you a certain conception, a presumption, if you will, of what professional librarians do and the means of and reasons behind doing it.

Global firms advise on a disproportionate amount of high-value, press-heavy corporate law transactions. These are the deals that drive the capitalist world economy, so they are naturally major concerns of political and business leaders. They are big-time and prestigious and they feel it.

Although the home offices often take the lead in deal management and accrued status, it is easy for all the firm's lawyers and business services staff to be swayed by the plentiful resources and vicarious prestige. Reputation is a powerful asset among service firms. The eminence of one's parent organization can be pervasive. One can imbibe it simply by virtue of one's status as an employee.

The professional self-image shaped by your workplace will guide the criteria you apply when considering "industry-standard" trends and imperatives. One might be tempted to believe that the business or practical priorities held by one's own firm are representative of law firms as a whole. With all that globally connected influence and coordinated know-how attached to the firm "brand" – and thereby to you – you might get the notion that your type of firm is the ideal form. However, this image of firm mission and method likely differs from the one held by the far more numerous practitioners at mid-sized or small local firms. Librarians are not immune from this potential slide toward hubris. The fundamental competencies and service goals of most firm librarians may be very similar, but how strategic, budgetary, and operational issues are played out in the daily work space can vary considerably depending on firm size and clientele.

Legal and regulatory issues

Significant developments in the law can have an impact on firm librarianship. This can happen in two ways. One: new and "game-changing" regulations can directly affect how the business and practice of law are carried out. Two: sweeping changes in an important jurisdiction's laws can increase the amount and nature of legal work that counsel has to contend with. Granted, neither of these occurrences would alter how firm librarianship is essentially practiced. They are more like additional environmental objects to be navigated and taken into account. Also, the first event's influence on the library profession is difficult to ascertain in the short term, even if it is immediately transformative on lawyers themselves. Still, to remain aware and effective, librarians should contemplate the eventual effects of weighty legal developments on their field.

An example of the first event is the passage of the United Kingdom's Legal Services Act in 2007 (see *http://www. legislation.gov.uk/ukpga/2007/29/contents*). The act contains several key measures but the one most relevant to future law firm practice is the authorization of alternative business structures, "which will allow lawyers to form partnerships with non-lawyers, and accept outside investment or operate under external ownership" (The Law Society, 2011). This has ramifications for traditional views of the client relationship, and changes in ownership and stakeholder interest will create thorny ethical issues of accountability and confidentiality. The business of law could be recast since "management of legal services delivery in the UK will become the partial domain of the corporate sector, which has a far more entrepreneurial view of market expansion and business development than most lawyers do" (Furlong, 2010).

Furlong (2010) also pointed to another effect of such legislation: "Corporate law firms could float shares on the stock market or invite private-equity investment, putting the proceeds into talent, technology, marketing or infrastructure to improve their competitive position." And in response to the Australian legal market allowing outside ownership, one firm did just that. Slater & Gordon became publicly listed on the Australian Stock Exchange in 2007 (Wenig, 2007).

In the United States, however, the legal industry has remained resistant to even partial non-lawyer ownership of firms. In April 2012, the American Bar Association's ABA Commission on Ethics 20/20 decided: "Based on the commission's extensive outreach, research, consultation, and the response of the profession, there does not appear to be a sufficient basis for recommending a change to ABA policy on non-lawyer ownership of law firms."[8] Among the primary concerns were the perceived negative effects on professional self-regulation and on the attorney-client relationship.[9]

In the US, the passage of the Dodd–Frank Wall Street Reform and Consumer Protection Act in 2010 (commonly referred to as simply "Dodd-Frank") (*http://www.gpo.gov/ fdsys/search/pagedetails.action?browsePath=111%2FPUBLIC %2F[200%3B299]&granuleId=&packageId=PLAW-111 publ203&fromBrowse=true*) is an instance of the second event. This piece of legislation brought expansive changes to the nation's financial system, primarily through its banking and securities laws. The Act itself runs to almost 850 pages, but it is the regulations needed to implement its provisions on a substantive level that is at the heart of its legal and procedural complexity. Several federal agencies (the Securities and Exchange Commission, the Board of Governors of the Federal Reserve System, and the Commodity Futures Trading Commission) have been tasked with implementation. Many rules (proposed and adopted) have been issued. Administrative guidance, political criticism, business industry commentary, and lawyerly analyses have been voluminous. The result has been a piece of legislation with massive and unforeseen consequences for the economy's architects and movers – banks, investment funds and advisers, institutional investors, and credit card, insurance, and consumer finance companies.

Since these major players are the loyal clients of large law firms, the implications for attorney workload are obvious. New and ambiguous risks, unsettled regulatory interpretation, and stricter oversight and transparency requirements mean greater reliance on proven firm expertise. Attorneys need to digest more information and exercise more diligence in identifying the legally relevant interrelationships that will touch upon their clients' interests. In response to Dodd-Frank and other legislation (such as Basel III)[10] enacted in the wake of the 2007-2009 global financial crisis, some international firms have likely realized the value of recalibrating their established practice groups to offer a more globally coordinated service for clients facing this new and unsettled regulatory regime.

As I stated earlier, it is difficult to distill the eventual effects of developments such as the UK's Legal Services Act on firm librarianship. I personally cannot foresee any real impact on the field's service ethic or its day-to-day retrieving and organizing objectives. Perhaps I am not much of a futurist. A widespread turn to alternative business structures could lead to a more efficiency-minded firm management. Law firms might be taken further in the direction of streamlined, ultra-competitive business-development enterprises. This could mean an undervaluation and shedding of librarian roles. But that might not be much of a novel predicament since, under the current partnership model, firm librarians are strangers to neither perpetually defending their value nor cost-cutting staff reductions.

For the second type of event above, the response of the firm library community is more apparent. Admittedly, Dodd-Frank is a legislative outlier. Not since the securities acts of the 1930s have there been such foundational legal changes to the American financial system. We are not likely to see similarly transformative legislation any time soon. But, as an extreme example as it is, Dodd-Frank underscores the duty of librarians to stay informed of the regulatory developments crucial to the work of their firm's practice groups. For librarians who regularly conduct business research, it has expanded their knowledge resources and the responsibilities for mastering them. To put the most current and on-point material in the hands of their attorneys, firm librarians need to know how to pinpoint the Act's interpretations in the many secondary sources that address it. The amount of coverage from treatises, law review articles, and news stories can be overwhelming. Lawyers themselves have been particularly prolific in their published commentary. Publicly available law firm memos and client alerts on specific aspects of Dodd-Frank number in the thousands.

Aside from its effect on the amounts of content to be reckoned with, such a monumental act of law-making forces firm librarians to maintain a healthy consciousness of their surrounding information environment. Administering the knowledge relevant to their service mission is an emergent process. In law and business, important changes can come from many directions, sometimes from several different sources at once. They can be convoluted and indefinite. Their outcomes are often cloaked by layers of reiteration and amendment. Because of this, one must be faithfully aware of the broader field and be prepared to swiftly respond to its reconfigurations.

Professional support lawyers

Some larger law firms employ professional support lawyers (PSLs). "PSLs are qualified lawyers who, for whatever reasons, have chosen to give up fee-earning work and taken on a support role which can include...drafting standard documentation or templates, assisting and advising the firm's fee-earning lawyers, [and] collecting know-how from lawyers and summarizing its content" (Harvey, 2003). They appear to be more common in UK and European firms than in American ones. Although PSLs often perform tasks that are closer to knowledge management, they have the same education, legal qualifications, and client dedication as lawyers with hourly billing requirements. Firm librarians will not see much difference in their reference encounters with them.

Interestingly, Harvey (2003) refers to the professional support lawyer as "the biggest threat to the traditional information professional in law firms." From my personal experience working in a firm that uses PSLs, I have never perceived PSLs as potentially supplanting librarians, and neither have any of my colleagues. Also, I am a regular reader of information industry commentary and news stories but I have yet to come across any item that indicated a trend toward cutting librarians and transferring their work to PSLs. Maybe such a move is too cost-prohibitive, since PSLs are licensed attorneys and, though their compensation is less than fee-earners, they do get paid more than librarians. But their productive co-existence with information professionals could be attributed to their utility. As Durrant (2006) states: "The nature of the work of a PSL often means they are information-hungry and therefore provide a useful bridge between the information unit and the legal department."

Outsourcing

Outsourcing is the contracting out of a company's activities to third parties in order to reduce costs or increase efficiency. It is usually assumed the work will be sent to a jurisdiction outside the company's home country. For many workers and politicians, it evokes strong emotions regarding job loss. For businesses, it entices with promises of increased savings and streamlined operations. Outsourcing does have some potential to be a future threat to firm librarians, although how much of a threat and the form it will take is hard to determine.

Its manifestation in the law firm environment is known as legal process outsourcing (LPO). It involves having legal tasks such as contract drafting and trial preparation support performed by outside vendors instead of in-house employees. LPO also calls forth conflicting opinions and conjectures. As Lin (2010) wrote, "there are few neutral observers." Some see LPOs as "the vanguard of a long-awaited and much-needed revolution." For others, their growth has "fed apocalyptic visions of a hollowed-out US legal profession in which fresh law school graduates find themselves competing for scarce jobs with young Indian lawyers willing to work for less than a tenth of what an American first-year associate makes."

The fact that legal process outsourcing is a relatively new industry and still developing also makes for contrasting interpretations. It has experienced consolidation (Deloitte Consulting, 2011), represents "a wide range of business models" (Lin, 2010), and is facing the challenge of diversifying its services beyond its traditional strength of litigation support (Fronterion, 2011).

Other complicating factors that work against a clearer sense of LPO's repercussions include:

- A reluctance of firms to publicly admit they are using LPO (Fronterion, 2010) due to concerns over competitive advantage as well as the obvious fear of political fallout (Robertson, 2011). It is difficult to make a reasoned judgment concerning outsourcing's extent if many projects are carried out in secrecy. This would preclude getting an accurate estimate of how many firms actually outsource and the nature of the operations they turned over to third parties.

- An apparent tendency of the legal and business press to rely heavily on LPO spokespeople for industry overviews and predictions. Many quoted forecasts come from self-interested consultants and the outsourcing firms themselves. While this might be simply an example of seeking out those with an informed perspective (Who would know the industry better than the insiders?), it runs the risk of blending marketing spin with objective assessment. Often, the result can be inflated growth projections and an exaggerated sense of the industry's vitality.

- The recent phenomenon of law firms developing their own service centers of back-office staffers in lower-cost regions of their home countries, leaving their fee-earning attorneys and managers in the firms' major offices. This is sometimes called "onshoring" or "insourcing."[11] Staff can be relocated from their former locations or recruited from the service centers' local markets. These new operations are also hiring lawyers, though at much lower salaries than their big city counterparts. The equally recent step of several LPO companies establishing centers and support services in American and British cities is further complicating people's preconceptions of outsourcing as a movement of jobs from developed nations to emerging economies (notably, India).[12] The move is a response to market and client demands, legal restrictions on performing some types of work overseas, and logistical efficiency.

For firm librarians especially, the ambiguity surrounding the impact of LPO on their field is even thicker, since most of the case studies and forecasting focus on LPO's effects on lawyers or back-office functions such as document review and billing. This lack of analysis may mean the firm library community has been relatively insulated thus far from outsourcing's more dramatic displacement effects. Perhaps a few firms here and there have contracted out their library operations and this slipped by the media. Or maybe the mainstream stories simply subsumed information work under the "back-office" functions to which they always refer. In any case, if there has been a salient impact on practicing librarians, it has been largely unreported as such.

Legal process outsourcing is a forceful trend in the law firm market and its implications need to be confronted. While the impression is that firm lawyers harbor doubts about the quality of outsourced work (Sachdev, 2011), there is also a general feeling that LPO is a permanent trend (Purzycki, 2012; Clay and Seeger, 2012), even if one is skeptical of its representatives' overstatements. It is perceived as delivering impressive cost-savings and its current domestic expansions attest to its versatility. Additionally, there are indications of in-house counsel's growing fondness for LPO (Collings, 2011). In financially leaner times, law firms are more responsive to the cost-cutting exhortations of the general counsel of their client corporations, who lately have been exercising more bargaining power in their dealings with external legal advisers (Green, 2012).

For law firm librarians, outsourcing is a vaguely threatening trend that appears to be steadily building. Its ambitions to broaden and provide more diversified legal services are forthright even if observers are hampered by the reluctance of firms to announce their turn to LPO. As a large firm librarian, I have some nagging fears about LPO's encroachment on my profession, but they are not acute. More instances of library-specific casualties need to be reported before my anxiety levels are noticeably raised. However, I do have a few opinions:

- There is the often-declared observation that the library community has always contracted out its most basic clerical tasks. That is, while not technically "outsourcing," this established practice has used local staffing agencies to provide such arrangements as filers for updating loose-leaf treatises or assistants to bar code and check in print publications. Any more expanded turn to LPO will likely affect technical services functions first. Tasks such as subscription maintenance and invoice processing are seen as most amenable to being automated and centralized by an off-site staff.

One possibility is that this contracting out of administrative workflow will be considered so successful that firms will send out the rest of technical services to third-party service centers. Catalogers and acquisitions librarians might follow, leaving only a handful of researchers to embody the "library." If the firm's reference librarians have already become almost entirely Web-based, the repercussions on their environment (and morale) might be minimal. But many firm libraries still have much-consulted physical collections. Print titles are still common despite an increasing number of electronic subscriptions, and they demand vigilance by experienced people who are professionally vested in their maintenance. At the hands of a remote service team, perhaps making programmed and perfunctory office visits, the collection could suffer neglect, eventually leading to an unreliable set of resources. A law firm collection requires faithfully updated titles; otherwise it becomes useless, counterproductive, or even dangerous for the attorneys who take its authoritativeness and currency for granted. It is debatable, but I believe that, to continue being of value, a firm library needs a dedicated in-house staff comprised of both reference and technical services personnel. If the attorneys' knowledge goals are to be met, the library staff needs to work closely and constantly with the collection, with the processes specific to the local office and the firm as whole, and with each other.

- A trend to keep one's eye on is LPO's apparent movement toward expanding the scope and level of its services, which could ultimately include high-level legal research. At present, outsourcers (and insourcers) do provide research, but judging from the shallow news reporting, it tends to be routine. Intellectual property searches and the creation of company profiles are examples of these basic operations. This type of information work often involves a pre-selected set of databases, highly standardized retrieval methods, and results formatted according to vendor-and-client-specified templates. If legal process outsourcing limits its research menu to these less sophisticated items, reference librarians should not lose any sleep over its advancement. Accomplished firm librarianship is a blend of experience, intelligence, creative adaptation, and an unflagging capacity to identify the right kinds of knowledge from diverse fields. Fairly simple reference questions from attorneys are regular occurrences – but so are cognitively formidable requests. An intellectual challenge is never far away. At times, one feels that some younger lawyers are simply forwarding their research assignments to the library (ones they should be tackling directly). Such reliance speaks volumes about attorney confidence in their librarians' skills at returning client-serving, on-point information. Third-party providers would have to invest copious amounts of time and effort to prove themselves worthy of such an elevated standard of trust.

Coming from a firm librarian, my glowing endorsement of firm librarians is partisan and might be an expression of wishful thinking rather than informed judgment. After all, it is conceivable that LPOs at short notice will begin offering viable legal research services that generate significant interest from law firm decision-makers. Some of the commentary is ominous, even if only dimly.

For example, Masur (2010) states: "As the LPO industry matures, however, the nature of outsourced legal work is expected to ascend the value chain." Another report mentions that one firm's onshoring move "specifically referenced its intent to hire local lawyers to bolster its research capacity in the new location" (Hildebrandt Institute and Citi Private Bank, 2012). The encroachment may be in the form of so-called "career associates" or "permanent associates," qualified lawyers who are paid far less than their fee-earning peers but also put in fewer hours and do not shoulder the same partner-track expectations (Rampell, 2011). Firms hiring these "second-tier" associates might perceive them as a cost-effective market for competent legal researchers. They have the education, training, and perspective to provide expert reference, although how many of them would remain for long in a position understandably seen as a "glorified librarian" is another matter.

A noteworthy development in this area was the acquisition of Pangea3 by Thomson Reuters in late 2010 (Thomson Reuters. 2010). Pangea3 has been called the "the largest 'pure-play LPO' company in the world" (Agrawal, 2012). Thomson Reuters is one of the two biggest providers of legal research content (the other being Reed Elsevier, parent organization of LexisNexis). Potential clients could perceive an outsourcer with insider access to the legal industry's most relied-upon knowledge platforms as a viable research hub. Firms might presume that the intimate availability of such key resources would translate into expert research with substantially lower search fees, especially if this allowed them to curtail their in-house research done on costly databases. As the custodian of the firm's high-priced databases, the library is usually perceived as the bearer of their cost to the firm. Though not reasonable, some partners or executives may equate the library with the price tag. It would be tempting to see a third-party service provider with in-group ties to such valuable databases as a path to substantial savings.

From my experience in large firms, the library supports the critical information needs of attorneys and their clients with a speed, effectiveness, and cadence that would be difficult to match by remote contract workers. Research prowess is important but there is a lot to be said for the motivating potential of being an in-house staff member dedicated solely to the firm. One serves as an officially employed professional with benefits, an anchoring physical presence in the home office, and a name and face recognized and esteemed by the firm's lawyers. Under this structure, there is a gratifying immediacy and connectedness to the librarian-attorney relationship. The staff librarian can reflexively respond to the idiosyncratic needs and approaches of several practice groups and dozens of individual lawyers. There is also a considerable amount of goodwill that any service-strong library will accumulate. Off-site attorneys-for-hire would be several layers removed from where the action is. This bodily disconnect from the flow could weaken those people's standing as integral co-workers, in their own minds as well as in the impressions of fee-earning lawyers. Again, this is the opinion of a firm librarian himself, and I am partial.

However, the lack of a catalyzing bond between the firm and the contracted legal researcher could very well be a tolerable trade-off for the firm director or senior partner enthused by the anticipated cost savings of workers earning less pay, receiving no benefits, and requiring no office space. This prospect of budgeting less for health insurance and matching retirement account contributions would be even more enamoring if the ones making the decision to outsource had little experience with the library's services and capabilities. In that case, absent any strong objections from influential attorneys who can attest to the library's value, the in-house reference librarian could be struck from the ledger.

- Legal process outsourcing is a nascent industry provoking much speculation, trepidation, and hype. Another prevalent response is diffidence. If numerous people have considered its implications, they have taken a wait-and-see attitude. Some librarians have reacted with the standard mantras: "Persuade them of our value! We must be seen and heard! Present a compelling business case!" O'Grady (2011), for example, encourages practitioners to be ready to argue the library's provision of "core business activities," defined as those that "support the strategic value of either the product delivered to the firm's clients or is core to the growth and development of the business." This is a decisive stance that can raise positive awareness of the library when it is needed most. But, considering that such a conscious self-presentation of value is already ratified as standard business practice for librarians, in good times and bad, it may not matter much if a budget committee is already sold on the merits of contracting out.

- Maintain a healthy cynicism toward those who define outsourcing as just another form of delegation.[13] The application of such a euphemism can be disingenuous, as it is often done by those with something to gain from outsourcing's expansion – or else nothing to lose. Also, do not accept uncritically the assertion that libraries have always outsourced, therefore it is nothing new and should be extended the same casual acceptance it has always received. While librarianship's historical use of third-party staffing for its clerical needs is uncontested, it is outsourcing's potential to encroach beyond routine administrative tasks, into the domain of credentialed librarians, that represents an unprecedented peril. Research and technical services librarians sense for the first time that maybe – just maybe – their professional positions could be fundamentally de-valued and stricken from the legal profession's accounts, never to return.

- One can admit that law firm use of legal process outsourcing is a good business decision for many firms while remaining heedful of the fact that third-party contracting could be detrimental to librarians as a professional group if its use was to substantially increase. Acknowledging real gains in efficiency for the parent organization does not preclude one from recognizing and criticizing the trend as a probable threat to the integrity of one's calling.

The intensity of the threat will depend on the future diversity of services offered by the LPO industry, the number of firms actually signing up and then renewing their arrangements for these wide-ranging services, and the overall amount of firm business that will be given over. Until I sense something more tangible – credible indications that my job will be outsourced to Bangalore or on-shored to Bristol (or Wheeling, West Virginia, for that matter) – I favor a wait-and-see attitude.

Knowledge management

Contemporary law firms create and analyze far too much information not to institute systems to effectively manage it. The practice of law is basically the expert application of legal knowledge to resolve social disputes. Although law in general is an information-intensive pursuit, the more complex the nature of a dispute, the more complex will be the information needed to understand and remedy it.

The large firm's caseload consists of a sizable amount of sophisticated transactions, so it is challenged with categorizing, analyzing, and preserving enormous quantities of information. The value of knowledge management (KM) comes from its systematic recognition and distillation of the relevant information that will serve a firm's practice and business goals.

Librarians, particularly at larger firms, do not have much choice when it comes to meeting the challenges of knowledge management. For the past several years at least, KM has grown into a very prominent feature of information work. In an important sense, this rise can be traced to the same business and technological developments that have stimulated the turn to KM in many organizations. Proponents continue to cite KM's competitiveness-enhancing capacity in a data-inundated world, but Internet-enabled communications and information creation, retrieval, and storage have proliferated to the point where setting up formal systems to administer them has become a prerequisite for everyday functioning. Moreover, as Rusanow (2003) makes clear, the fact that law firms are learning organizations operating in a knowledge-based market where "the law is constantly evolving" makes firm culture an excellent fit with KM goals.

Knowledge management is much more than the simple application of technology to a firm's collected information items. In this book I will not cover the prevailing theories of KM or the best practices for implementing a KM program.[14] But it is important to stress that KM is a sophisticated, ongoing, and often expensive operation that embraces an entire firm. If the firm's reach is global and its information sharing is properly integrated, the investment in personnel, time, and resources can be immense. Because of librarians' central role in both internal and external information handling, their involvement in knowledge management on some level is a given. It may be direct and official, with some librarians hired as full-time KM administrators or "web services librarians," or it may be a lesser job function, with some librarians performing traditional reference duties but having additional intranet editing and indexing responsibilities. But even if not directly participating in the organization of internal firm knowledge, librarians will be expected to be capable finders of it.

To better grasp how librarians interact with knowledge management in law firms, it is useful to perceive KM as interfacing four variables: people, culture, technology, and documents.

People. Any effective KM system requires a formally appointed staff to coordinate it, establish procedures for adding new items and removing those flagged for deletion, and act as the go-to people for technical assistance or policy guidance. Although attorneys wield final authority over content and access levels, the KM administrators control how and when a document is uploaded to the system. As editors and architects, they possess the most comprehensive intelligence regarding an item's location and metadata. It is therefore crucial for librarians to maintain a positive relationship with them. They are insiders to an estimable source of information. Frequently, you are at a loss for retrieving a specific document even after applying your most formidable arsenal of search skills. When that occurs, the KM person will be able to tell you if that item is actually on the system and, if so, how it can be accessed. As responsive information professionals themselves, they will often send you the item directly. Retrieving on-point internal know-how is a common request. Working closely and amicably with KM staff can greatly extend the reach of one's capability for delivering firm-produced knowledge.

Culture. The worth of a KM system is judged by how well it enables the systematic sharing of actionable knowledge. To have real value, the firm that administers it must foster a collaborative organizational culture. Staff members need to be willing and able to share their know-how but, just as importantly, there must be robust top-down policy support for participation. A wide range of information items is necessary for the practice and business of law. Attorneys need ready access to all of them, barring any restrictions due to confidentiality concerns. They also need to know that the posted information is current and relevant. Such a culture of contribution and a system of expert personnel and credible documents calls for a committed management.

Firm librarians – qua librarians – are presumed to have a natural familiarity and dexterity with anything pegged as "information" by one's co-workers. This applies even for material that has little to do with law or business. Access to any article, report, or survey, no matter how embedded behind a subscription pay wall, is the library's supposed bailiwick. Following this logic, they are expected to be accomplished users of the KM system. They will often be the initial contact for such requests from anyone who has relinquished their own erratic browsing for the smart searching of trained professionals. Because of this reliance, librarians will turn to the system's contents for a more diverse array of resources than most others in the firm. Such dependence means librarians must hold the same nearly-unquestioned confidence in the integrity of the system's information that they have in the authoritativeness of databases published by major vendors. That level of assurance stems from the backing of a diligent and reputable administration. The firm culture must demonstrate that it strongly endorses a policy of information openness and reliability. Installing a KM system that lacks a threshold of comprehensiveness or that fails to check for outdated items is a wasteful undertaking. Sophisticated judges of information trustworthiness such as librarians will be frustrated in their attempts to extract useful knowledge and soon abandon it. For attorneys, relying on such material can be perilous if it is used as grounding for legal opinions.

Documents. Law firms are document-concentrated organizations. When I refer to a "document" I mean any information-bearing item and not the traditional conception of a paper-originated record in paginated form. A document can be a case decision, a scholarly article, or a joint venture agreement as well as a spreadsheet, a directory, or a screen shot of a web page. It can be in electronic or hard copy formats. It can be born digital or a hand-written manuscript converted into a scanned image. According to this definition, all organizations are based in and around documents. However, law firms boast a uniquely intimate relationship with documents. Their raw work materials are the legally compelling documents that are brought to bear on people's lives through the invocation of binding laws. The information-bearing items depended upon by attorneys are quite consequential. They can be designated as court-sanctioned proof of an action or intention, adjudicated as evidence that favor or obstruct a client's interests, or even cited as the legitimate exercise of a political body's will.

Ask any firm librarian: documents matter. When searching for them on a KM system, one should keep in mind the following characteristics about internally-posted information. These are particularly true for instances of know-how (documents such as legal memos, checklists, best practice guidance, deal templates, and training manuals that represent a focused embodiment of attorney experience and learning, recorded for the guidance of others faced with the same situations or facts).

- Most of a firm's document output will never be posted to the KM system in any form. Most of that output was never meant to be posted. Even if there is an explicit, management-sanctioned intention to post everything deemed relevant to the practice or business of law, any attempt to do so would fail miserably. The aggregated output is too vast and diffuse, spread across many departmental, practice group, and office silos, and lodged securely in the heads of unidentified and possessive individuals. It is also unrelated and unlinked by an established taxonomy or classification scheme. Most imposingly, it would be in constant need of supervision and updating in response to its ever-changing law-and business-based environments. Such constancy could never be adhered to.

For any type of document you come across, you cannot know what other examples of that type (perhaps superior ones) are being held back, either because someone never bothered to post it or because a person had strong proprietary feelings about letting the world get a piece of their hard-earned wisdom. After all, it is natural to nurture the advantage gained from not releasing all of one's "secrets" for public consumption. A firm's emphasis on billable time and a professional culture that rewards individual drive and ambition means lawyers are not motivated to devote much effort to knowledge management activities.

- There is no way to know the scope or currency of a document unless the author or person responsible for posting it specifies its upload or revision date and includes a note indicating its properties, limitations, or any relevant metadata. Documents or web pages can be orphaned; that is, they can be left dormant and outdated for years because of neglect or the person responsible for maintaining them has left the firm.

- In some KM systems, responsibility for maintaining individual intranet pages is assigned to different staff members, based on subject relevance and expertise. These systems offer user-directed web authoring software so the individuals assigned to a page can edit it as they see fit. This arrangement's drawback is the differences in diligence and care that various individuals bring to the assigned task. Some will conscientiously maintain their pages. Others will be remiss. One advantage is that each page's last revision will be date (and perhaps time) stamped and the assigned editor's name will often be noted. This allows anyone interested in the page's contents to contact the editor for additional information.

- The KM system should not be relied upon for retrieving authoritative versions of external knowledge (such as statutes or regulations) that will be used as the basis for client advice. Always confirm with the originating external source (e.g., a government website) or a reputable aggregator (e.g., Westlaw or Lexis). It is impossible to update every example of primary law posted to the internal system and it would be flagrantly inefficient to try. When looking for valid law, the best practice is to seek out the most current version available from the most trustworthy source available. The internal system is not that source.

- Because of client confidentiality or an author's personal decision, document access can be restricted to staff members who have worked on the matter or have been granted access by the author(s) for some other reason. If enough documents are restricted in this manner, the intended benefits of a collaborative system may be lost. In fact, there is an ongoing debate among firms regarding the extent to which a document created for a specific client matter should be shared with those not directly involved with the matter. Many believe that such work product should not be shared at all. There is a fear that once a document is open to almost anyone in the firm, the nature of simple and instant document delivery via email makes it more likely to be forwarded outside the organization. Those with a restrictive view of document control perceive a real risk of violating client confidentiality or a potential for the firm's competitive edge to be weakened through wide dissemination of "trade secrets." Any currently generous re-use of firm know-how would recede if such a view becomes the norm. Both attorneys and their librarians would lose a valuable source of knowledge.

Technology. The notion of knowledge management as synonymous with information technology is common. With the spread of computer networks into every facet of society, IT has come to be perceived as infrastructurally foundational by business and the public. Internet-based communications are conspicuous drivers of knowledge building; therefore the domination of popular consciousness by technical features is understandable. However, one should not reduce the key components of content, policy, and process to the apparatus that facilitates them. Like the closely interacting components of people, culture, and documents that together constitute KM, technology is necessary but far from sufficient.

In law firms, this technological manifestation is found in the document management system (DMS) and the intranet. The document system, sometimes referred to as an enterprise management system, is a database of indexed and searchable work product, usually memos, agreements, and guidance created by lawyers in the course of a particular client matter. Access rights are set by firm policy and document authors. Even if most of its documents are open to all, the majority of the system's users will be attorneys and, to a lesser extent, librarians and other support staff who search it on their behalf.

The DMS is distinct from the firm's intranet, which can be accessed by every employee and contains a much broader range of document types and information. This locally loaded internet is the firm's central communications portal. In many organizations it has become the only viable platform for current and comprehensive employee awareness, internal contact information, and departmental insights.

In addition to including documents from the DMS that have been cleared for public consumption, the intranet can include policy handbooks, internal and external directories (e.g., of recommended foreign counsel), legal topic pages, bound volumes (the documents of completed client deals centralized and searchable from a single interface), and practice group sites with standard agreement templates. If the firm is large enough, its intranet can contain an all-embracing global intranet and links to regional or office-based intranets with information tailored to local needs.

For librarians in global firms, the intranet is a ubiquitous presence and a perpetual source for requested information. Because the intranet has become the de facto as well as the official provenance of basic employee information, the items uploaded to it are often current and in effect. However, when retrieving matter-based work product or externally-produced material, it is important to remember the characteristics of internally-posted information that I bulleted above.

Notes

1. Law firms can be solo or group practices. They can also take on business structures other than partnerships, such as proprietorships, limited liability companies, or professional associations. Merriam-Webster defines a partnership as "a legal relation existing between two or more persons contractually associated as joint principals in a business" (*http://www.merriam-webster.com/dictionary/partnership*). Its key feature is that the partners share ownership and profits as well as any legal rights and liabilities, although personal liability and management duties are circumscribed in so-called limited partnerships ("LLPs"). Laws regarding the nature of partnership can vary according to country. For a good overview of the nature of law firm partnership in the United States, see Chapter 3 ("Law Firms and Partners") of Munneke (2003).

2. For an analysis of the similarities and differences of different types of professional service firms, see Von Nordenflycht (2010).

3. Cornell University's Legal Information Institute offers useful overviews and examples of jurisdiction (*http://www.law. cornell.edu/wex/jurisdiction*), subject matter jurisdiction (*http://www.law.cornell.edu/wex/subject_matter_jurisdiction*), personal jurisdiction (*http://www.law.cornell.edu/wex/ personal_jurisdiction*), and territorial jurisdiction (*http:// www.law.cornell.edu/wex/territorial_jurisdiction*).

4. Although client matters drive the time and efforts of attorneys most of the time, they also require research support for non-billable matters, such as article writing, assisting in business development presentations, or getting up-to-speed on various legal or business topics.

5. When referring to large firms, I use the terms "global" and "international" interchangeably. Some authors distinguish the two. Mayson (2008), for example, uses these two terms, in addition to "multinational," to "suggest three different strategies in the evolution of global legal practice." Such granular distinctions would be too distracting for my purposes.

6. Baker & McKenzie – Firm Facts (*http://www.bakermckenzie. com/firmfacts/*).

7. Not all librarians bill their time. It depends on the firm, the particular client arrangement, and even the geographical location of an office within the firm. US-based firm librarians are more likely to have their time billed than their European or Asian peers so, for example, the Chicago librarians of a global firm could bill their research hours while the Barcelona librarians of the same firm might not.

8. See press release, "ABA Commission on Ethics 20/20 Will Not Propose Changes to ABA Policy Prohibiting Nonlawyer Ownership of Law Firms," available at *http://www.abanow. org/2012/04/aba-commission-on-ethics-2020-will-not-propose-changes-to-aba-policy-prohibiting-nonlawyer-ownership-of-law-firms/*. For the resolutions and reports of the ABA Commission on Ethics 20/20, which is performing "a thorough review of the ABA Model Rules of Professional Conduct and the US system of lawyer regulation in the context of advances

in technology and global legal practice developments," see *http://www.americanbar.org/groups/professional_responsibility/ aba_commission_on_ethics_20_20.html.*

9. For the perspective of several general counsels of major corporations, see "Comments of Nine General Counsel on the ABA Commission on Ethics 20/20's Discussion Paper on Alternative Law Practice Structures," February 29 2012, available at: *http://www.americanbar.org/content/dam/aba/ administrative/ethics_2020/ethics_20_20_comments/nine generalcounselcomments_alpschoiceoflawinitialdraft proposal.authcheckdam.pdf.*

10. See "International Regulatory Framework for Banks (Basel III)," Bank for International Settlements, at *http://www.bis. org/bcbs/basel3.htm.*

11. See Rampell (2011), Randazzo (2011), and Qualters (2011).

12. See Timmons (2011), and Ring (2012).

13. Friedmann (2007), for example, says: "Lawyers have long delegated administrative functions to staff and to outside vendors. They regularly delegate substantive legal work to other lawyers, paralegals, and other professionals. Sometimes they delegate to lawyers in distant offices whom they've never met...Analytically, the idea of sending work offshore is not so different than delegating."

14. The many theoretical and practical considerations of creating and maintaining a knowledge management system in law firms is effectively covered in Rusanow (2003) and Parsons (2004).

4

The law firm library

Abstract: The ways of the law firm library are primarily determined by the practices and goals of the law firm itself. However, the library retains the characteristics of an information unit and a business unit, regardless of its role as a firm-anchored department. The most compelling of its duties as a business unit is to provide value to its parent organization. The library is expected to contribute to the firm's bottom line. The firm library community is alive with argument and agreement over the best methods of proving one's value, whether library value is amenable to established financial metrics or if the end point is better understood as the administration's acknowledgment of value in whatever form a particular library can offer. One mainspring of value is the library's effective handling of its budget. Major challenges intrinsic to library finances include the changing needs of its main user groups, the shifting balance between print and electronic subscriptions, and the struggle to recover costs from clients for research time and database access. Librarians are expected to take a direct role in managing contracts and licenses. They also engage in aggressive marketing practices on behalf of the library itself. Another organizational concern is a library's relationships with other offices and departments within the firm as well as with other library units. As information units, firm libraries are confronting the same trends as other types of libraries. A proliferation of formats has led to a re-conceptualization of the collection that goes beyond the library walls. Fresh approaches to service such as embedded librarianship are being explored. Also central to firm librarians' duties as information experts are their obligations to train their users thoroughly on work-critical databases and to monitor that staff usage for the sake of copyright compliance.

Key words: value imperative; business value; budget; finances; cost recovery; contracts; licensing; marketing; collection development; embedded librarianship; training; copyright.

As argued in the last chapter, the law firm's culture and structure exert a powerful influence on the methods of its library. Indeed, the firm and its library are linked to such an extent that it can be difficult to examine a library's operations without relating them back to the firm's sway. However, there are variables whose expressions are attributable to the nature of the firm library as either a knowledge service or as a business service, or a combination of the two. They are affected primarily by the practices of librarianship and business performance. They emanate from the firm library's role as the information management arm of a for-profit enterprise, and are relatively independent of the imprint of the law firm qua law firm. A case can be made for some of the environmental qualities described in this chapter as being traceable to firm culture, for its impact never recedes entirely. Nevertheless, I have tried to limit this section to those elements that firm librarians would regard principally as library or general business issues.

The library as a business unit

The value imperative

The practice of law is a tradition-rich profession dedicated to serving client interests while upholding the integrity of the legal system. At the same time, many attorneys carry on their vocation through profit-seeking business structures, namely, law firms. For highly trained professionals, this does not necessarily lead to a conflict of interests. Both revenue seeking and a fidelity to the demands of jurisprudence can be pursued (and attained) without contradiction. Both pursuits determine a law firm's character, goals, and strategies. However, maintaining an ethical stance can seem the less arduous undertaking. Though not without its unexpected and sometimes severe pitfalls, adhering to the canons of professional responsibility is rather straightforward. The truly challenging task is constructing a viable business model that generates consistent revenue while offering clients a valued service – and maintaining this successful equation in the face of unyielding changes in one's environment.

A firm's choice of business model and how resilient it remains are beyond the concerns of most librarians. They are the provinces of finance executives and senior partners, so I will not cover them in this book. However, a firm's general financial health is tied to the cost-effectiveness of its individual departments. Each unit is expected to control costs (if not increase revenue) and, above all, to demonstrate its value. Such value is defined in terms of its business value, that is, the service or utility it provides uniquely or most efficiently that contributes to the firm's long-term success. There must be a business case in support of keeping a division or department as an ongoing budget item. A firm library is certainly no different. It has to regularly present its case, particularly if it is well funded. In other words, as a recipient of firm resources, it must justify its right to exist.

Dealing with special libraries such as firm libraries as if they are business assets – or as potential assets waiting to be duly recognized and exploited as such – has been a recurring theme in the library field for at least a century. Handy (1912) made a strong case for the library's value but only if it was taken seriously and nurtured by the parent organization: "When business shall treat it as it treats other factors of business success, discerning its possibilities of usefulness, encouraging and planning for its development, adapting it to the requirements of business activity, then it will justify itself unquestionably." A hundred years later the idea of value for librarians has taken on much larger significance and a sense of urgency. The commercial enterprises that employ them not only perceive their business value but now demand constant proof of it.

Firm librarians have progressed from feeling the need to regularly direct management's attention to their value to being nearly obsessed with punctuating it at every possible moment, lest they quickly be consigned to obsolescence. Librarians newer to the trenches cannot remember a time when ardent self-promotion was not an integral part of the job. Veteran practitioners may have been in the field when it was less of a marketing crusade, but memories of those moderate times are likely faded and nostalgia-steeped. The present mood of constant, barely submerged anxiety seems to predominate.

The globalizing, technology-suffused business environment brought unprecedented competitive pressures, consolidations, and downsizing in the past two decades. But the international financial crisis of 2007 and subsequent recession made cost-cutting an inflexible norm. Immersed in social networking and a 24/7 media in multiple formats, many people (perhaps so-called knowledge workers most of all) began to experience a heightened consciousness of economic fragility. Librarians were not immune to this sensitivity. There was a general apprehension that unemployment or stark times could be just around the corner for almost anyone. Rationally or not, the system is now seen as fundamentally inauspicious for the "average" working person. And the presumption is that it will persist unchanged for quite a while.

These real events and their crowdsourced translations led to librarians adopting a collective attitude of self-preservation. They wanted to ensure their true value was properly recorded. It was the best, the only way to escape the shadow of departmental purging. The drive to prove themselves was further stimulated by a library community apparently engrossed with the theme of vocational siege and the workable strategies its members could wield when facing it down. The anxiousness and somber perceptions are still in abundance. A muscular advocacy of value remains the library field's call to arms.

Such is the value imperative's centrality and re-iteration that one suspects it has taken on the power of an occupational meme. Focusing attention on it is a valid response to a foreboding era, though referencing it is sometimes done as a matter of convention. Dramatically portraying the imperative and creatively grappling with it can serve as a functional script for engaging one's community of practice. A shared discourse of struggle is cognitively unifying.

Experienced commentators have maintained a spotlight on the imperative's governing sweep. Regarding special libraries in general, Matarazzo and Pearlstein (2011b) affirm that "Corporate librarians and their libraries are critically evaluated all the time. This close and continuing evaluation and the need to prove value every day are constants." Addressing law firm libraries in particular, Egan (2008) advises: "Librarians should make efforts to communicate that their position is not a center of expense but a center of value. This is accomplished by tying library service to a valuable revenue stream ... the idea is that the library is part of the success of the revenue stream."

These judgments and the ensuing calls for proactive business case-building have struck a chord with many librarians. In light of its potential to motivate, I doubt such a strenuous frame of mind is going to languish any time soon.

Library academicians, consultants, and practitioners have been looking into the topic of how parent organizations assess library value for quite some time.[1] However, dedicated coverage of law firm libraries in this literature is lacking. Most of the relevant discussion revolves around the special library as a general class. Treatment of this broad library type is relevant to those interested in firm libraries, since many special libraries share key features regarding their user relationships and collection development objectives. But firm libraries retain enough distinct characteristics that extrapolating from these broad studies should be done only tentatively.

Firm libraries often struggle when called upon by management to translate their value into the standard outputs of business. Most of their firm-enhancing contributions appear resistant to the methods of quantification sought by the business-minded. Granted, the library has always kept reliable statistics to maintain control over both its departmental and task-related efficiencies. These have usually reflected customary library measures like circulation counts (how many times a title has been checked out), received reference requests, and database usage according to number of logins or searches. Most libraries are also faithfully budget-conscious and take very seriously the charge of controlling expenses while increasing effectiveness.

However, those who require true business value solicit a stricter standard of numerical representation, manipulation, and benchmarking. The types of metrics that administrators expect of the things and processes they administer, such as return on investment, cost savings per unit, and expense ratios, can be daunting to those who prefer to express their professional worth in narrative rather than in numbers.

Perhaps the firm librarian's discomfort with metrics reflects the legal profession's own uneasiness with them.

Kilroy (2012) describes the profession as believing that metrics "provide a reductivist view of an activity which involves complex interactions that aren't really capable of or susceptible to numerical measurement, such as the giving of legal advice." Expert counsel, like expert knowledge services, is seen as a dynamic qualitative asset. It is assumed to be too humanly complex to be stretched across the Procrustean bed of data compliance.

This natural reluctance to numerical measurement is overcome in practice because it frequently has to be. Harsh economic realities sometimes compel an unforgiving profit-seeking approach. Or management insists on applying a standard metric because it is the organization's normal way of tracking costs and the library must align itself like any other supporting unit.

Firm librarians confront the value imperative with an earnest intent to satisfy its demands, but they naturally ask: how do we measure this value in the first place, given the intangible nature of many library services and their often overlooked contributions to value? This can pose a challenging set of obstacles for librarians hoping to promote their worth.

After all, the value imperative suffuses the entire firm library's outlook, perhaps that of reference librarians most of all. Reference work brings one the most exposure to a distinctly monetized notion of time and task. It is value-driven with a constant concern for prompt, relevant, and cost-effective results, but the proof of this value is usually difficult to pinpoint. Research value is realized when a question is answered and a lawyer's or client's issue is successfully resolved – and the librarian's service has facilitated the resolution unobtrusively. The most impressive results are those accomplished without exposing the workings of the infrastructure without which the result could not be attained. The firm client does not see the librarian's input because it requires only the expert counsel, delivered by an attorney as a unified end product. The *client's* inattention, however, is not problematic for the librarian. It is the obliviousness of the lawyers that will lead to trouble. As Furlong (2012) claims: "The problem is that lawyers tend to shrink or cut anything whose function or value they don't really understand. So if your lawyers don't clearly understand the work or perceive the value of your library professionals, you've got cause for concern."

Studies on the value of special libraries acknowledge the difficulties presented by this unsettled measurement issue. However, they accept it as part of the natural terrain and treat it accordingly. Though explicit references to law firm libraries do not appear in them, these studies nonetheless provide firm librarians with a valuable foothold for demonstrating their value in business terms. They give insight into management's thinking on the topic and introduce the language necessary to claim its attention (at least initially). Such surveys are a great source of industry views on library best practices and proven strategies for comprehending and conveying value in a for-profit setting. As such, they should be heeded by all special librarians, firm librarians included.

Considering the insights in the studies above in light of my own professional experiences, I offer the following observations on value:

- Differences in firm size, culture, and managing policy can result in firms taking very different paths to value assessment. Different firms will demand different metrics, and some of them will be less business-oriented than others. Even within a single firm, especially if it is global, the libraries in different geographical regions of the firm might be held to varying standards of value measurement. Much depends on the particular administration overseeing the budget. If the library is tasked with choosing one or more value metrics but has limited guidance on this choice from firm executives, their choices "should reflect what library management knows about the parent organization's leadership and how they think." (Strouse, 2003).

- The decision-makers a library reports to might require strict performance measures – but not ones to be implemented by the library itself. Ratios could be calculated by regional directors using basic variables submitted by the library. More traditional figures like the cost of salaries, subscriptions, and materials would be compiled by librarians and passed on to administrators on a regular basis. Librarians would carry only the initial burden of collecting field data and avoid the more complicated formulas of later-stage budgeting. Library size and the positioning of the library within the organizational structure have significant ramifications. Larger libraries have their own managers or directors to oversee their operations. These positions entail high-level responsibilities, including financial planning, allocating, and budgeting. They are more likely to perform the more rigorous budgetary analyses themselves. A smaller library, in contrast, may be officially designated a part of the information technology or marketing department and might have little to do with applying sophisticated metrics.

- Notwithstanding the refined fiscal instruments of senior managers and directors, many metrics are beyond the reach of most practicing librarians. They lack the training, experience, and resources to adequately carry them out. At times, the valuation of a special library might be perceived as best handled by outside consultants who specialize in such matters. Reliably expert valuation involves a substantial amount of time and effort, things the in-house staff, even those in the finance department, might not be willing or able to provide. Hiring an external firm can be a large expense that management refuses to approve, but the real hitch is the long-term commitment needed if one is to maintain an accurate and actionable representation of the library's value. The firm library contains a dynamic mix of hard and soft variables that fluctuate according to their transactions with the firm as a whole. A single capture of this value profile will be valid for only so long. A dependable assessment to be used by management in short-term planning as well as in strategic plans compels a constant recording and measurement. Employing an outside expert on a regular basis could be considered too expensive, despite the long-term insights to be culled. But calling a consultant in only once might be seen as inadequate for gaining real perspective and not worth the cost. However, even a single expert valuation has definitions, methodologies, and observations that can be referred to in future situations for empirical guidance.

- There is a need to always reflect on the strength and perceptions of the library's value in addition to expressing it, even if the expression is not done in business terms. As Housewright (2009) argues, "Simply choosing to measure value and to adopt a value-oriented mindset lays the groundwork for corporate library success... The self-evaluating library will be better prepared to demonstrate its value in terms meaningful to management." Such an outlook attests to a proactive and business-minded concern with value, which communicates an image of the library as responsible and cost-conscious. This can lead to a powerful wellspring of goodwill from both lawyers and management.

Always focus on materializing the value requirements of library work and advertising their positive implications for enhancing the firm's bottom line. The traditional tallies of librarianship can be endorsed in the absence of more stringent financial ratios. One significant source of value is the budget savings realized from continually evaluating digital and print subscriptions for their usefulness. Weeding hardcopy titles and cancelling unused electronic databases can trim sizable costs from the budget and confirm the library's reputation as a department of effective professionals.

- Strive to maintain a record of specific achievements that underscore the library's value. Verbal testaments add substance to numerical metrics. "Case studies that relate the use of information to meeting business goals can make empirical evidence seem more real." (Ryder, 2011). These can be short narrative accounts by lawyers or business development managers that highlight the library's contribution to a research question or project. The occasional testimonial furnishes a short burst of self-esteem. But enough of them, compiled in a folder and received from senior lawyers and partners, can be submitted to management at performance review time as a type of supportive evidence.

Positive feedback can be complemented by such performance measures as surveys and interviews, although such measures have limitations in a firm setting, where time restraints are always major issues. Of the two, the survey is more likely to be employed, frequently as part of an overall survey of business services. Survey feedback is often respected by managers as a valid indicator of library value. It is an effective barometer of customer service satisfaction and the favorable responses, sometimes signed by the individuals and quite laudatory, can enhance the library's perceived value on at least that important dimension.

Opinions in the published literature vary as to the extent to which the value of special libraries can be measured and communicated in standard business terms. All recognize the challenges of quantifying information services: the stubbornly intangible aspects of knowledge work and the murky cause-and-effect path between a librarian's answer and the firm member's use of that answer in accomplishing tasks and adding economic value to the organization. A library's impact on daily operations, let alone on long-term productivity, is entangled in countless layers of interpretive ambiguity. If not shelved as a lost cause, however, the goal of disentanglement might be supplanted by a more creative set of techniques. For example, He, Chaudhuri, and Juterbock (2011) provide a good example of innovative possibility in their discussion of the Novartis Knowledge Center's Value Assessment Library Use Efficiency project. Matthews (2002), on the other hand, begins his book-length exploration with the various forms of evaluation and measurement that special librarians should be aware of when navigating issues of value, perhaps for the first time. He concludes by advocating a balanced scorecard approach, fine-tuned for use by special libraries.

It is important to keep in mind that even axioms regarding a library's handling of value issues – those that elicit the response, "Of course you have to do that! There's no other way if you want to survive." – might not be attempted in practice, even if they present themselves as options. As stated before, how a library measures value and who does the measuring is affected by firm size, culture, structure, and executive praxis. But perhaps the most beneficial advice for firm librarians is to maintain a deep-set appreciation of the regard their organization's decision makers have for value. It is an obligation that managers expect others to share. Consequently, to show a strong dedication to the firm's value creation through proficient and engaging projects is to build up the library's credibility as a worthy asset. Putting the department's monetary value on paper via industry-standard calculations may not be as pivotal as manifesting its commitment to value in a library-appropriate manner that administrators nonetheless still commend. "Although interlinked, value and the perception thereof are separate concerns, and the latter is perhaps more significant for securing support for the library." (Housewright, 2009)

Budgeting and finances

The law firm is a profit-seeking organization. Controlling costs, increasing revenue, and reducing inefficiency are among its most sought-after goals. Providing the best possible service to clients is the firm's overriding objective, but such a provision would not last long if the provider were not as attentive to its business interests as it were to its professional duties. For firm libraries as for all other departments and the parent company as a whole, an ongoing attentiveness to one's finances is a fundamental business necessity.

Maintaining a responsible budget is identified so closely with the value imperative discussed above that budgetary accomplishments are often subsumed under it as a natural sub-division. However, in its significance to an organization's basic functioning, the budget stands apart. It must be addressed independently of the imperative, no matter how deeply implicated it is in a department's value profile.

Although responsibility for the preparation, oversight, and presentation of the budget is assumed by a library manager or director, and many staff librarians will not even set their eyes upon it, the library's finances are an ever-present factor for everyone. It is a tangible marker of the library's reputation as a professionally responsible member of the firm team, so to speak, and most staffers are aware of this representation. Because of its perceived use by administration as an easy-to-read surrogate for the library's value, the effective management of the budget is a continuing concern for all library personnel.

The financial governance of a business unit with a sizable budget is a complex affair. It calls for robust managerial skills that transcend any one occupational setting. Budget managers need to be adept at planning, allocating, forecasting, monitoring, and valuating. These competencies are frequently invoked in combinations that practitioners can apply in effective measure without necessarily being able to explain how the combinations and applications are performed. That is why such skills are complemented by proven experience. The library anticipates and responds to the present and future resource requirements of the firm, particularly its various practice groups and client focuses. In such a dynamic context, it is crucial for budget creation to have the major input, if not the actual authority, of an experienced librarian with a mature grasp of the field. Appropriately, Maher (2006) stresses the awareness component of a library's financial planning. That is, for the library to adequately chart its fiscal course it must stay attentive to the evolving needs of its users and how information is delivered to them, to the structure of its own organization and its place within it, and to the external environment of legal publishers and vendors, whose products and services are in constant flux in both minor and transformative ways. Even if the budget is in the final hands of a non-librarian, its successful administration is contingent upon a tacit and penetrating knowledge of the industry. This can only come from the extensive advisory contribution of a practicing firm librarian.

Firm library budgeting includes several of the items most budgets cover, regardless of organizational type. Among these common variables are staffing salaries, physical space (for libraries, this encompasses offices, the print collection, offsite and onsite storage, reading areas, and the reference desk), and administrative basics such as office supplies and services. In a library or non-library setting, these major items are treated similarly. However, firm libraries present several finance-related challenges that implicate all the planning, monitoring, forecasting, allocating, and valuating duties of its managers, often simultaneously and in different degrees, depending on the budget item.

A distinctly challenging item is the unfixed nature of the library's collection, both in its print and electronic formats. The collection has two points of instability, each of which can arise independently of the other. Each point requires management to be prepared to amend or modulate its allocative, monitoring, and valuating operations, frequently without fair warning.

One is the impact of practice group changes. As I have discussed earlier, the content of a firm library's collection is determined by the practice groups that serve a particular office. Such groups grow and diminish (or dissolve) according to legal marketplace demands and firm or practice area management capabilities. Sometimes, entirely new groups are created if the firm believes the market could profitably support them. Additionally, some groups become engaged in projects that require more information resources and library research assistance than other groups, so they will place more demands on the staff and the collection. The ebbs and flows of practice groups must be accommodated by a relentless planning, monitoring, and re-allocating of the library's resource usage.

A second reason for instability is the ever-shifting balance between print and electronic formats. Publishers are increasingly turning to digital versions of print resources. Often, both formats are retained, with the electronic format being updated far more quickly as well as being preferable in terms of its search functionality and downloading and printing features. The catch is that publishers are bundling the two formats into higher-cost packages, which are unavoidable because there are enough lawyers in the firm who demand either one or the other. The electronic versions are more sophisticated research tools and have become the norm for newer generations. However, there are still large numbers of veteran practitioners who have made their venerable hard copies an integral part of their work flow. Keeping track of who uses what resource, how often, and how successfully adds a complicating layer to the oversight obligations of librarians.

A collection with numerous print titles also forces extra monitoring and allocating efforts in that different titles are updated according to different publication schedules and pricing schemes. Depending on the publisher and the subject, some treatises are updated weekly, others monthly, still others quarterly or annually. There are loose-leafs, single-volume treatises, and multi-volume series of primary law and encyclopedias. Some are priced as premium products and can have hefty subscription fees. Books can be updated with pocket parts or stand-alone pamphlets, or replaced with brand new editions if the publisher deems the pocket part already too bulky (or if the new edition can reliably bring in more revenue). This variation in pricing and invoicing can make collection management a laborious project in a library boasting multiple subscriptions with many suppliers. The stress can be intensified by publishers who decide to dramatically raise the price of a subscription service when it is time for renewal. The new offer might be unreasonably high. But, then again, all of the attorneys have become dependent on it. It is one of the firm's indispensable resources. Let the vexing contract negotiations begin...

Cost recovery

Cost recovery is a basic undertaking of all professional service firms. Firms seek monetary compensation for the time, materials, and labor costs they incur in the process of advising their clients. Recovery policies vary between firms. Most are set by formal client agreements, although supervising partners have wide latitude in writing off many client charges and a good deal of informal give-and-take negotiations influence the final recovery numbers.

For firm librarians, cost recovery comes from charging the client for transactional use of databases (i.e., searching and downloading) and for the librarians' time in utilizing those databases or other resources, such as the print collection or the Internet. Again, the extent of charge-back for both resource usage and library time varies with the firm and the client. Some firms install clear recovery policies for both resources and time; others do not bill any library time and categorize all database charges as firm overhead.

Established recovery programs are significant parts of the budget. The librarians administering their departments' finances need to incorporate recovery expectations and realization into their planning and monitoring actions. Most front line librarians will not be privy to the recovery arrangements of their firms. These are usually the domain of top-level managers and partners. However, since library-based cost recovery is a fairly common practice, especially in larger firms, it is wise to keep informed about it.

There are general recovery issues that will be unavoidable in everyday reference work:

Client matter numbers. Legitimate charges cannot be billed to a client if one does not have the matter number assigned to that client. Sometimes a lawyer will give a librarian a practice group number in lieu of the billable number if he does not want the client billed for any research or database costs. Or the matter may be new and not yet assigned a system number, though attorney work on that matter must begin immediately. Nevertheless, it is good business practice for librarians to habitually ask for a matter number when taking on an assignment. Librarians have no control over the matter numbers they receive, and most firms have not set minimum billable hours for librarians, so they should not fret over being given mostly non-billable practice group numbers for their research time.

Client validation programs. To ensure recovery of transactional database costs, libraries have worked with vendors to implement software that requires users to input recognized matter and attorney-identifying numbers. The databases will not allow access without these numbers. Legal work is beset with time constraints. It is tempting to quickly enter a database – especially one that remembers the user's sign-on credentials – without having to pause to enter a cumbersome set of digits. Sometimes the attorney simply does not want to bill the client for online research and wishes to skip the matter input stage. However, for recovery as well as budgetary and administrative purposes, major transactional databases should force the user to enter a matter number, whether billable or departmental.

Cost recovery computations for some databases can be confusing. Librarians are often asked by attorneys about the actual client cost of a search or document download. Unfortunately, librarians are sometimes unable to provide an unequivocal answer. Again, this might result from the different and unknown charge-back agreements for each client. It might also reflect the complex calculation methods used to determine the percentage of a database transaction cost that will be passed on to the client. The major subscription services such as Lexis and Westlaw have multiple pricing arrangements. No two large firm contracts are exactly the same, although as institutional buyers with frequent, heavy users, such firms usually sign a minimum monthly usage agreement with set pricing and discounts based on the amount of their actual usage. Suffice to say, the contractual language that addresses a firm's transactional costs can be difficult to decipher for many librarians, that is assuming they even have access to the contracts. The cost recovery assessment can be even more confounding if less than 100% of the firm's discounted price is charged back.

Keeping an accurate tally of one's time for every reference task is not an instinctual behavior for librarians. Despite being entrenched in a work environment where billable time is a hallmark, librarians will probably have to repeatedly remind themselves that the hours and minutes it takes to answer a query, large and small, must be scrupulously recorded. Remembering to record one's time is particularly challenging when deeply involved in a lengthy, complex search. It is all too easy to lose track of the passing hours when immersed in such an absorbing task.

Librarians have some individual discretion for what tasks to bill for and to what extent. Some jobs are completed so quickly and routinely that, despite firm policy indicating they should be billed, are considered too negligible to charge for. Some research work, especially if the subject area is new and complex, can take significant amounts of time. For a librarian, there may be some reluctance and a sense of guilt to bill for that much time if it seems inordinate. It is common to self-interrogate: "Should I have taken that long? It seems unreasonable." Librarians also contend with discretionary practices that might be out of their individual hands. Gediman (2012) touches upon several recovery factors that librarians should be familiar with, such as "Are the various types of research treated differently?" and "Does each practice group treat recovery differently?"

Librarians' billable time is sometimes written off by partners in response to client objections or in anticipation of a protest (and a desire not to rock the boat, especially if a client's bill is already high from attorney time charges). Such actions are very common and should not be taken personally, although in everyday practice in large firms, librarians have no idea when and how frequently such write-offs occur. To help minimize the possibility of such revenue losses, Waremath and Kaczorowski (2008) offer worthwhile practical tips that can "improve, energize, or augment" a firm's existing recovery program.

Contracts and licenses

The proliferating digitization of legal information has led to a corresponding growth in the use of electronic license agreements and bundled contracts covering both digital and print services. Content coverage is prodigious and the copyright and legal implications of access are numerous if not always fully understandable to all parties. Contractual arrangements between law firms and vendors are now complex, highly negotiated, and invested with appreciable sums of money. Firm librarians, in maintaining their traditional roles as architects and strategists of their firms' collections, have developed beyond being simple contract keepers. They are engaged contract managers. Although participation in license initiation, negotiation, renewal, and cancellation is frequently limited to managers and directors with the assistance of firm counsel, librarians are increasingly involved with some aspect of their firms' contractual obligations. As credible advisers on practice group interests, they can offer guidance at the formation and renewal stages on whether the agreement's provisions and limitations serve the firm's needs. They can also actively monitor staff members' compliance with a subscription's terms of service.

Contract administration comes with obscure legal terminology, diffuse intimations of copyright liability, and an insistent call for negotiations with people often shrewder and more aggressive than the average librarian. As such, it is one of the more stressful and unpalatable features of firm librarianship. Success at it might even be a matter of temperament. Some practitioners never become comfortable with the process. However, competence at evaluating a contract's strengths and weaknesses in light of what is beneficial for the firm – becoming adept at recognizing the elements of a "good" contractual arrangement – can be gained from direct experience and the mentoring of a senior librarian. In an excellent survey of the relevant issues librarians will confront while licensing digital resources, Harris (2009) underlines the importance of an open mind and knowledge of one's institutional objectives: "Knowing your library's goals, understanding the clauses that appear in licenses, and entering into the negotiation process with a flexible view and authority from your library will result in licenses that meet your needs."

Marketing efforts

Like contract management, active marketing of the library's value is a salient feature in the development of firm librarianship. These promotional efforts are necessary even in a less frugal era, since proving one's business value is a natural imperative of support units in any for-profit organization. But as economic times have gotten leaner and firms more ruthless in their curtailing of "spend," law firm librarians have been on the defensive. Reacting to the threat of being perceived as an unnecessary expense, they have put forth a blueprint heavy on earnest self-marketing. The aim is to capture the attention and win over the sober minds of the so-called "C-suites," the chief executives or finance officers who determine final budgets.

Few would deny that the current business environment requires a sustained effort by librarians to publicize their value to lawyers and funders. The methods (and the beliefs motivating the choice of those methods), however, tend to vary considerably between firm libraries. Some libraries insist on vigorous branding efforts whereby every research action is prominently stamped as a library product. To further this purpose, some libraries have enlisted the assistance of in-house design teams to create original logos. Newsletters, sponsored training events such as lunch-and-learn sessions, and regular feedback surveys with receptive follow-up are a few of the more common ways of getting the word out and circulating the image.

The expansion of marketing efforts among law librarians has both drawbacks and positive outgrowths. One of the vulnerabilities is a credulous faith in marketing's unmitigated effectiveness. To aggressively promote one's library services has grown into a type of dominant ideology. It is assumed to always be a testament to one's professional cogency. The reality is that, in the absence of well-crafted studies or reliable feedback mechanisms, the effects of most marketing methods are indiscernible to library staff, particularly in the long-term. And such structured studies and feedback are probably not the norm. The positive repercussions of a promotional project is presupposed in the same way that marketing in general is thought to be efficacious in an automatic, ambient way. Another difficulty of the marketing agenda is that the driven frame of mind it sets in motion requires a steady supporting stream of time and resources, things which a scaled-back library staff will find very challenging to maintain.

A beneficial side effect of the marketing push is that it forces law librarians to take a long, hard look at their places in their organizations. It compels a healthy self-assessment and attentiveness to the library's perceived value. If that value is discovered to be lacking, promotional energies lead librarians to a closer engagement with lawyers, their principal clients. And that is definitely salutary. Additionally, since marketing is a business-minded practice, those who take the time to learn its techniques could gain a more cultivated business sense, something that is quite pragmatic in a for-profit enterprise.

If one's firm is constructing a budget in an atmosphere preoccupied with financial soundness through trimming and streamlining, marketing projects, no matter how dedicated and "in the flow" they are, can be unavailing. Doubling one's promoting efforts during downturns may not add much extra punch. However, if library marketing is judiciously carried out in good times and management does take notice, it might serve as a repository of goodwill to draw from during harder times.

Relationships with other departments, other offices, and other library units

The library is part of a system. It is one business service among several in a legal organization where the goal of all departments is supporting lawyers who serve firm clients. Such a fact is obvious and unremarkable, if hardly ever examined in full. Librarians need to be cognizant of the importance of recognizing and cultivating the relationships it has with other firm units. For some of these other internal departments, you may not have even realized that a relationship existed – or that it existed in a neglected state and could yield benefits if acknowledged and worked on. Realizing that one has a functional relationship with these other staff members is a first step. The next step is the meaningful one: Reaching out and identifying each other's objectives so that each party can offer its peculiar perspectives and tools for the attainment of the other's objectives. This teamwork and reciprocity are conducive to the smooth functioning and success of the library and the firm as a whole.

Accomplished interactions between a firm's units, where each one responds with comprehension and courtesy, is a necessary condition of its continuity. "A 'one-firm' collaborative approach among administrative departments is necessary to compete in the current legal market" (Stemlar, 2008). An ethos of cooperation also reaps benefits directly for the library. Among its most visible relationships are those with the departments of information technology (IT), marketing, and business development. There are advantages to be gained from taking a collegial stance toward them. A major one is the positive image the library will be displaying to decision makers. As Matthews (2012) puts it, "Most firm management groups will look favorably on joint projects; so while you, the librarian, won't be the 'rock star,' you will get credit for supporting departments outside the library." He points to the valued reputations that marketing and business development departments have for improving the bottom line and how the library could secure some of it through well-publicized joint projects. Success with these projects would provide "the business context that most law libraries need their services to be associated with."

An advantage of being a librarian in an international firm is that you are part of a tight network of fellow librarians (or information officers, depending on the location). Firms with practice groups and offices located throughout the world engage in cross-border transactions that implicate the laws and practices of multiple jurisdictions. These large, complex deals require the contributions of many different attorneys from various legal backgrounds and practice specializations. The librarians who provide the information to complete these deals are also spread across the globe (or at least across a country). And like their lawyers, these librarians also connect and assist across borders. This might be called a global reference network, where jurisdictional expertise is delivered at point-of-need through electronic communication and professional affiliation. Although some firms have adopted a model along the lines of "a centralized digital reference desk staffed by two dozen researchers in numerous time zones" (see Chessler, 2011), the norm is to reach out to library teams individually when given a question that involves foreign law. If a London information officer receives a query regarding Delaware partnership law, the best move is to contact the New York library staff. The latter would know where to find authoritative material on this state (as well as on the other forty-nine). Of course, if the attorney request were time-sensitive, the gaps in the time zones might make a reliance on one's peers across the ocean impractical. Additionally, most firms do not have far-flung offices with well-staffed libraries. But librarians in large firms should appreciate the potential of this unique resource. As a high-powered internal listserv, its participants are always guaranteed to answer, even if the response is "Sorry, I can't help you with that one."

One valuable relationship often taken for granted but crucial to the performance of the library as a cohesive unit is the everyday collaboration between the reference and technical services departments. The research desk is perceived to be the library's public front, since librarians at the desk have the most direct interaction with attorneys. Even if reference staff members are not recognized by face, their names can be very familiar to lawyers from the numerous emailed requests and responses. However, despite being a rear-office region of invoices, books, and boxes, technical services is the library's vital nerve center. Its staff maintains the catalog, physically administers the collection, processes acquisitions and subscriptions, and handles the routing lists through which attorneys keep informed of consequential legal and business developments. On an operational level, fostering professional interdependency and mutual respect between reference and technical services should receive priority over similar efforts directed at other administrative departments. For the library's value as the firm's locus of knowledge stems from this underlying symbiosis between its basic components.

Library hierarchies: managers and directors

A firm's staff size, number of offices, and geographical reach will impact most of the library attributes I discuss in this book. My work experience is in libraries connected to global, multi-practice firms, so my examples and observations will reflect this background. One variable worth mentioning is the library's management structure. Solo practitioners might shoulder most of their libraries' administrative, contractual, and budgetary obligations, with support and final approval for major decisions given by an office manager. Libraries in mid-sized firms might have a manager with considerable authority to sign off on large contracts and the autonomy to run the library as seen fit, although a chief financial or operating officer or a managing partner will retain oversight when it comes to material firm business. The largest firm libraries could have a director and several managers or supervisory librarians, perhaps one presiding over reference and one in charge of technical services. Nichols' (2008) description applies to many global firm libraries: "Often the director is the bureaucrat of the organization and does not tend to be a research practitioner, focusing more on the operational and strategic elements of running the department." The managers under them continue to perform research tasks, maintain the catalog, and develop the collection, but spend substantial time taking care of the library's day-to-day staffing and policy needs.

The library as an information unit

The goal of any library, no matter what its organizational setting, is serving its users' needs through the organized provision of information. This section will address several of the firm library's salient properties related to information handling and delivery that aspiring firm librarians need to be aware of. Their distinct configurations are affected by their strategic locations in the law firm environment, but they are general properties of contemporary librarianship that will be universally recognizable by most practitioners.

The expanding definition of the collection

Traditionally, a library's collection was equated with its physical holdings. These were predominantly books but could also be maps, audio and video recordings, or any type of tangible information-bearing item found in a "special collection." The turn to electronic resources and their remote digital distribution altered the understanding of a "collection." It came to be comprehended as "information resources for which the library invests financial resources - directly or indirectly – to manage, service, or preserve on behalf of library users, regardless of the location of content" (Association of Research Libraries, 2002). According to this increasingly expansive definition, public websites, physical resources held by other libraries, and articles obtained via document delivery services are parts of the collection if the library provides the material means (e.g., computers, network or wireless connections, and order-processing staff) that enable users to access them.

Commercial vendors aggregate vast amounts of content and license access to it on a provisional basis. For some librarians this digital transformation was an uncomfortable reminder of the distinction between ownership and access. But the old notion of a library holding legal possession of the bulk of its knowledge is no longer tenable in a world where it is more efficient and cost-effective to lease or freely download valuable information. And though disparaged by a few librarians as an encumbrance to the full, unmitigated grasp of their institutions' stock-in-trade, the abundance of information found outside of library possession has been accepted without second thought for quite some time. Limited access and full ownership co-exist in the same institutional space with little controversy. Even a decade ago this situation was unremarkable to both librarians and their patrons. "The norm is now an interdependent mix of ownership and access, with the location of the material increasingly irrelevant to users" (Association of Research Libraries, 2002).

One interesting development of this is the change it causes in the library's acquisitions function. Formats have diversified to the point where the ownership of many of them, especially the content-profuse electronic database, is beyond the financial means of the library. In response, "the mission of acquisitions has changed from acquiring things to connecting with content" (Holden, 2010). That is, collection development now calls for a proactive recognition of the interplay between access, service, and purchasing in the fulfillment of user needs. The availability of large quantities of content in multiple formats is not a revolutionary situation for most people, least of all for librarians. However, the evolving procurement and access environment presents a set of facts that will keep metamorphosing, most likely in unpredictable ways. Upholding a professional level of responsiveness requires a consciousness of its possible implications, rather than a simple acknowledgment of its existence and the reactive stance that goes with it. Holden discusses the transformation from the perspective of a technical services librarian in a university, but it will affect law firm librarians as much as any other library practitioner.

The library as a service

Providing information has always been one of the library's cardinal attributes. Lately, however, there has been more emphatic talk in the law library community that equates a library's defining identity almost exclusively with its service ethic. In other words, a prodigality of content has made the information-bearing items themselves secondary to the librarians who create and perpetuate the pathways to those items. In a knowledge universe where researchers fluently move between the free and the fee, it is the facilitative skills of librarians, no matter their physical location, that becomes their most impressive value proposition. Lambert (2012b) nicely distills this belief when he states "the idea of the Law Library as groups of three-foot radiuses of services." He argues that firm librarians, whether conversing face-to-face in attorney offices or out of sight behind a computer screen, can serve their users with expertise conveyed with "the reach of the human arm." Librarians are mobile "bubbles of services," less beholden to their books and work stations than ever before.

Embedded librarianship

One of the consequences of the library as a service has been a burgeoning interest in embedded librarianship. This practice has been pursued in one form or another for several years by academic and medical libraries. Its implementation by firm libraries came later, although they probably have been employing various dimensions of embeddedness for a while before the term started to gain currency. In a way it is like knowledge management (KM), a fresh-sounding concept that embraces well-established practices but re-purposes them with a more contemporary mission. Unlike KM, its advocates have not disseminated many explicit definitions. However, embedded librarianship is understood to involve placing one or more librarians in a direct working relationship with a specific user group or department, where the librarian(s) will offer specialized, targeted information services. The services are the same that libraries offer to their general population of users (current awareness, competitive intelligence, database training, and resource discovery) but an embedded practitioner will deliver them in engaged and sustained interactions, often in close physical proximity and resembling a constructive relationship more than a series of encounters. The result is a quicker and deeper understanding of the specific group's needs and a more sophisticated expression of the library's value.

Depending on library type, organizational size and culture, and management styles and beliefs, embedded librarianship tends to be defined, promoted, and evaluated differently. But it can lead to unmistakably positive consequences for firm librarianship. Among them are:

- Increasing the visibility of the library at the everyday field level of attorney awareness. This close interaction could countervail any drift toward librarian invisibility and suspicions of irrelevance that come from reference communications being conducted almost exclusively via email and phone (Adams, 2012).

- Giving the library better insight into the particular information needs of different practice groups, which will improve its acquisitions decisions as well as give it more confidence and effectiveness when managing subscriptions, from commencement to renewal or cancellation (Gebauer, 2011).

- Promoting a more open and fluent exchange of information with the firm's major practice areas could eventually cultivate the knowledge health of the firm overall if the group end products were transferred to established knowledge management practices and systems.

- A conviction by lawyers and management that an embedded program is successful creates a measure of good will for the library that can be put into operation for future value-promoting activities.

One barrier to embedded librarianship is the need for initial executive and lawyer buy-in. Depending on the firm, this can be welcomed as a first-rate idea or dismissed as a waste of time. Even with a supportive administration, setting up such a program can require daunting amounts of perseverance, planning, and social capital from librarians, which may be difficult to assemble if the library is understaffed. And once a program is initiated, it demands top-level advocacy and practice group cooperation on an ongoing basis.

A challenge to maintaining long-term results is the potential for overextending the reference staff, particularly if the program is auspicious and the powers that be decide it should be extended to multiple practice groups. The program may be too successful for its own good. If one's office has several practice areas and a relatively small research staff, the possibility for vitiating the program's effectiveness by spreading the staff too thin is very real. Of course, if the library can afford to dedicate a few of its researchers exclusively to one or a handful of departments, they can focus their energies fully on these targeted user groups. But because budgets are nowadays curtailed, chances are the embedded librarians will still be performing their customary reference duties. Ideally, they will be addressing the varied information needs of the rest of the firm with the same responsiveness and thoroughness they commit to their specialized groups. In a resource-bounded environment, embedded librarians could discount their universal value by fragmenting their time and labor and spreading them unevenly among discrete user groups.

Training

The information needs of attorneys are now furnished primarily through electronic resources. Some of these can be used intuitively by anyone familiar with a computer windows interface and mouse. The more specialized and content-heavy databases demand a higher investment of time and patience to learn. Firm librarians are continually on the lookout for new and worthy digital sources and then setting up their trial subscriptions, evaluating their usefulness, and alerting lawyers to their availability. But their primary responsibility is training staff on the multitude of databases the firm subscribes to. The library maintains the contracts and password lists attached to these subscriptions, although to the attorneys these are remote activities irrelevant to their knowledge tasks until they misplace their log-in credentials. Real value comes from the instruction the librarians give that will allow practitioners to seamlessly integrate the resources into their daily work flow.

Vendors often assign dedicated customer representatives with training expertise to large firm subscribers. They hold group and individual instructional sessions for incoming associates and set up periodic refreshers for password holders wanting to brush up on their skills. For high-end commercial databases with copious content, sophisticated functionality, and big price tags, vendor provision of specialized trainers has become routine. The service obligation owed to major clients speaks for itself. However, vendor representatives are just as important from a functional standpoint. They have a deeper understanding of their own products – the basic features as well as the bells and whistles – and can answer questions about its capabilities and most recent additions because that is all they know (and I mean that in a positive way). Their allotted training time is restricted given the comprehensiveness of the databases they are demonstrating, but they can tailor the session to the practice group or professional interests of the trainee.

One thing vendor-supplied trainers cannot – or will not – do is advance cost-effective alternatives to their products. They are in your firm to give an overview of "Database x" or "Resource y." Their professional commitment is to "x" or "y." Even if they did have the solid practical knowledge of other, perhaps competing products, they are obligated to pitch for their own. Firm librarians are not tied to such corporate duties. They can summon up all their past interactions with a wide array of products and evaluate them according to the library's or the individual attorney's needs. Librarians know pricing, relative strengths and weakness in searching, downloading, and formatting functionality, and content ceilings (such as time embargoes on newer material and limitations on full text). A veteran vendor representative states it simply, "Librarians have the broadest experience with information resources. They are able to compare, contrast, make distinctions, note pitfalls and expand possibilities in *any* of their available resources based on their experience with *all* their resources" (Lowry, 2012; emphasis in original). Aside from its experiential robustness, library training is motivated by firm-aware and firm-directed concerns. It knows the organization's interests and it serves them. That makes it quite estimable.

Copyright issues

Copyright embraces the library in its roles as both an information unit and a business unit. It is a central and abiding issue. But navigating the legal, financial, and pragmatic terrain of copyright is among firm librarianship's more frustrating challenges because:

- Much of the law, in practice and in the judicial interpretation of the statutes, is decided on a case-by-case basis. How the facts and legal issues of these established decisions can apply to any one of your situations is often unclear, making compliance a formidable process. Confident understanding of the situation may call for involvement of a copyright attorney, which is often impracticable for everyday copying dilemmas.

- In terms of copying and disseminating, there are some things that you obviously cannot do and some things that you evidently can do. What gives rise to the most ambiguity and contention are the things you *might* be able to do or the ones that *perhaps* you should not do.

- Most of the copyright legislation and secondary literature on it seem to be written with educational institutions in mind. Practice-oriented analyses for the for-profit information professional – let alone the law firm librarian – are lacking. Two notable examples, examining United States copyright law in the context of corporate libraries, are Heller (2002) and Miller (2011).

- Copyright enforcement and legal interpretation involve Big Money stakes. The roiling of huge financial interests can be seen in the legislation being proposed and the lawsuits being filed (noticeably, by commercial companies and associations against allegedly infringing individuals). Media coverage and intellectual discourse spotlight the war of ideology between corporate rights-holders and those arguing for a less rigidly controlled copyright regime. It is understandable that a librarian would be intimidated by such a dramatically unsettled area.

- Firm and client business relationships have been globalized and implicate multiple legal jurisdictions. An international firm's intra-organizational reach often draws in several foreign offices with which the home librarian communicates. Sending various digital documents or scanned printed pages from different databases or publisher imprints brings up issues of domestic versus foreign licensing restrictions and the probability that each vendor treats copying and dissemination to parties outside of one's local jurisdiction a bit differently from the others.

- The intense time pressures of firm life make facile but illicit copying an easy temptation. Librarians are more aware of the restrictions on the material they send, but they are almost totally ignorant of what the attorneys actually do with the material once it is received. Some license agreements forbid forwarding to external parties, including clients, but allow circulation to fellow firm employees in foreign offices. Of course, there are additional limitations on whether those foreign staffers can themselves copy or forward the material. Their actions are even further removed from the attention of librarians.

- Widespread and instantaneous personal and network storage make illicit copying a lot easier and therefore more alluring. This increases the chances of legal liability because, as users take advantage of cheaper and better functionality through technological innovation, so do the publishers. The latter are installing more sophisticated rights management and tracking software in their products, enabling a more comprehensive monitoring and reporting of misuse. If user infringement is occurring regularly by others somewhere in the firm, this acute level of vendor surveillance can make managing compliance more stressful and time-consuming for the librarians designated by the vendors as main contacts for their subscriptions.

- The terms of one's licensing agreements will take precedence over one's statutory rights as promulgated in the copyright laws. And the library has multiple agreements with various vendors. Each license delineates different sets of usage and distribution rights and violations.

Because of fast-moving social and technological developments in copyright law, there are no reference-ready answers for the challenges above. One must be temporarily content with indefinite practice pointers. However, there are several things to remember that can lessen the chances of infringement.

- Librarians can be the firm's go-to people for copyright questions relating to database use and the photocopying of the collection's print publications. Importantly, the library should develop a compliance policy and have it readily available, if not posted conspicuously at the reference desk and next to any photocopiers in the library. But, the truth is closer to this: attorneys, if they do set foot in the library, probably do not pay much attention to compliance exhortations for such obvious things as copyright ("After all, everyone knows you can't make all those copies, right?"). Back at the attorney desktop, all that electronic copying and forwarding is just so easy. And time is limited, partners and clients are waiting, and hours need to be productively billed...

  One possible deterrent to the urge to uncontrollably copy is to regularly send out emails stressing the fundamental importance of compliance from a business perspective. These messages could refer to the substantial civil damages that the copyright statutes allow and the courts have awarded in the past. A case notorious for its enormous monetary penalties (and scare potential) is *Lowry's Reports v. Legg Mason* in a Maryland federal court (see Curle, 2004). These electronic communications can be supplemented with library-sponsored awareness seminars by external experts such as the Copyright Clearance Center (see next item).

- Larger firms often subscribe to so-called reproduction rights organizations. These are non-profit associations that broker compensated access to intellectual and creative content on behalf of creators, publishers, and other rights owners. They manage collective access to copyrighted material in all formats, ensure that royalties are properly dispensed, and foster more transparency and reliability in worldwide copyright compliance and remuneration. Such entities can be found in many countries. In the United States, the Copyright Clearance Center (CCC) (*www.copyright.com/content/cc3/en.html*) is by far the most influential. The United Kingdom's major players are the Copyright Licensing Agency (*www.cla.co.uk*) and the Newspaper Licensing Agency (*www.nla.co.uk*). A global listing of such associations can be found at the website of their umbrella organization, International Federation of Reproduction Rights Organisations (IFRRO), at *www.ifrro.org/RRO*. Both the CCC (*www.copyright.com/content/cc3/en/toolbar/education/resources.html*) and the IFRRO (*www.ifrro.org/content/booklets*) offer informative reports and booklets on a wide range of copyright-related topics.

A license with the above associations can be very expensive, particularly for a business seeking copyright permissions on a global level. Small to mid-sized firms can be priced out of using them. However, they offer a centralized platform for quickly ascertaining a firm's copying privileges. Significant time and labor are saved by not having to contact numerous rights holders and then waiting for each of their replies – which, whether granting or denying permission, can be unacceptably belated to an attorney expecting to read an article forthwith. By partnering with a reproduction rights organization, a firm also builds a credible-reputation for good faith dealing in copyright matters, which may serve as an affirmative defense in cases of future accidental infringement.

- The courts apply copyright standards more rigidly to for-profit organizations than to academic and public institutions. This means that for corporate libraries such as those found in law firms, judicial determinations of infringement can be more readily found and higher punitive damages could be imposed. Judges come down hard on defendants that possess the assets to comfortably fulfill their information needs but who nonetheless willfully and frequently infringe for commercial purposes. The law also distinguishes between isolated, spontaneous copying and frequent or systematic copying. Needless to say, it looks more forgivingly on the former.

- Be sure you fully understand the meanings of the terms in your license, since they trump copyright law's provisions relating to use. Insist on plain language in your contracts. If this cannot be adhered to, or a few opaque clauses slip in, consult your manager, director, or firm counsel for guidance. Or confirm your understanding with the vendor itself. When in doubt, always strive for permission from the person or organization with the legal right to give it.

Notes

1. These explorations offer a wide range of approaches for understanding the issues involved in assessing and justifying library value, including review articles (Woldring, 2001; Keyes, 1995), surveys (Matarazzo and Prusak, 1990 and 1995), case studies (He, Chaudhuri and Juterbock, 2011), and theoretical analyses (White, 1979; Matthews, 2002 and 2003; Strouse, 2003; Sykes, 2003; Ryder, 2011). One research review, published by the Association of College & Research

Libraries, (2010) focuses on academic libraries in both title and substance, but contains a section on special libraries (pp. 82-92) that is well worth reading.

2. I apply the terms *budgeting*, *finances*, and *cost recovery* in a broad sense to give the reader an idea of the fiscal responsibilities expected of firm librarians. I also use the words *budget* and *finances* and variations thereof as if they are interchangeable. Managers with notable budgeting experience might strongly object to my conflation. They would likely cover each of these topics separately, applying finer conceptual distinctions and tracing detailed interrelationships between them. My purpose is simply to underscore the general financial ramifications of maintaining a law firm library. For a deeper (and better) analysis of this function, see Maher (2006).

5

The legal publishing world

Abstract: Firm librarians and lawyers are dependent on premium knowledge content for their professional needs. An inordinate amount of this information is controlled by a small number of private corporations. The top three global organizations are Thomson Reuters, Reed Elsevier, and Wolters Kluwer. Among the products they own, the most valued are the aggregated databases of premium content. Their comprehensiveness, quality, and functionality enable substantial time and cost savings. The legal publishing industry is experiencing a time of consolidation. The largest owners are active in acquiring smaller publishers to diversify their offerings and remain competitive with their peers. The competitive environment has also been shaken by a new major entrant, Bloomberg Law. To distinguish themselves, vendors are motivated to continually enhance their services. This has given the consumer an improved set of products though not necessarily a lower cost to access them. Law librarians do not have much power in influencing prices in such an oligarchic market, but they should be aware of the idiosyncratic pricing and access issues they face doing business with leading information providers. Among these is transparency in licensing terms, differential pricing, bundling of print and electronic resources, and the firm-wide versus individual password approach to subscriptions. In addition to the obvious benefits of a positive, resource-rich vendor relationship, librarians need to be attentive to its unexamined influences. The social psychological components of the relationship can unduly impact one's attitudes toward the overall value of the service, thereby preventing consideration of equally legitimate sources.

Key words: aggregators; competition; consolidation; customer representatives; legal publishing; pricing; training; vendors.

Legal information: the distinct value of aggregation

In a market-based society, the information-centered professions are dependent on the organizations that legally own the knowledge necessary for the successful practice of those professions. For firm lawyers and librarians the authoritative information needed to fulfill their basic missions is controlled by private interests. Legal practitioners rely on primary sources of law and the equally vital secondary sources that update, summarize, analyze, cross-reference, and consolidate those statutes, regulations, and official decisions. Both types of legal publication are essential to the provision of expert counsel. An increasing amount of primary law is being made freely available on government websites, and open-access journal and news articles are commonplace, but commercial vendors govern access to much of the premium content. Just as crucially, they control the technological platforms that most efficiently combine and manipulate that content.

Aggregators are enormous repositories of diverse content, assembled into a single searchable interface, for which the owners (often themselves referred to as "aggregators") pay licensing fees to the content providers and then charge subscribers for access to that third-party content. Usually there are different levels of access and pricing schemes, depending on how much content one wants to access and how large a contract one has with the aggregator (the bigger the customer, the better the discount). Large firms subscribe to at least one of these services, often two, and pay predetermined monthly fees at set rates.

Presently, there are many worthwhile information resources in circulation. To subscribe to or regularly purchase even a modest percentage of them would be inconceivable. For large law firms, the standard way of efficiently accessing the fullest range of relevant knowledge sources is by subscribing to an aggregating database. Aside from its profusion of content, its most compelling attribute is the vast savings in time and cognitive effort it affords its users on an ongoing basis.

The perceived advantage of such a service can be illustrated like this: "Aggregator A" combines twenty valuable information resources under a single interface. All are searchable alone or together. All are subject to the same versatile search, display, print, and download options. Those same twenty resources can be accessed via separate subscriptions to ten or fifteen smaller independent vendors. When bought separately, the combined cost of these multiple licensing agreements might be attractively lower than Aggregator A's pricing package, but it would also mean managing more and maybe very different sets of licensing terms, administering numerous passwords (possibly in a combination with some IP-authenticated firm access), and forcing one's attorney-users to constantly switch between multiple sites with varying search languages and levels of usability. The monetized time factor is immediately apparent. Additionally, there is the very real possibility that much of the content stored in the aggregator will only be needed occasionally. Taking out full subscriptions to pricey resources that are infrequently consulted can strain one's budget to the breaking point. This illustration uses the example of an aggregator that concentrates twenty resources. The biggest aggregators actually bring together *thousands* of different resources. And a large law firm may feel the necessity to browse many of them in its indefatigable search for on-point information.

Possessing access to everything an aggregator offers can be quite expensive. But, again, the time saved in simultaneously searching and downloading premium content is substantial. For those captive to the billable hour – and for the staff that responds to their queries – utilizing such aggregators is seen as a matter of professional exigency. The aggregator is also compulsory for the firm as a competitive enterprise. If one's peers are using a major aggregator for their research needs, and performing faster and more comprehensive knowledge work than those who do not subscribe, the non-subscribers are susceptible to a definite loss of competitive edge. For lawyers, often the most valuable content is the discrete piece of knowledge that conclusively settles a legal question. If it were lodged behind a pay wall on a small content owner's website, hidden from search engines, it may never be found. But, if it were aggregated in one of the common platforms, it could be retrieved and applied without hindrance. The practice of law would be that much more efficacious. Predictably, there is a striking tendency among legal professionals to ratify such integrated platforms as vital to their information existence.

There are numerous publishers of high-quality content. Some are small independent vendors; others are mid-sized or fairly large, but not on par with the largest few. They all create and distribute relevant law-related knowledge. However, the aggregator – a fusion of premium content and platform at a unified point of access – is a singular source of value in the legal information world. Both of these essential elements deserve some discussion:

- **Premium content.** Attorneys and librarians require unimpeded access to expert coverage by reputable authors and editors on a multitude of topics, mostly on legal and business matters, but potentially on any subject. They need to be able to search, compare, and contrast similar types of primary law from manifold jurisdictions, such as the banking laws from five separate states or territories. A diversity of secondary sources on a subject allows attorneys to gain a wider analytical understanding of those laws, such as how each jurisdiction's legal culture influences the current judicial or legislative reasoning behind its laws. Competent counsel stems from the breadth and depth as well as the authority of one's sources.

Premium content is represented by skilled reporting and analysis. It is the customary narrative expertise found in treatises, scholarly articles, news stories, and guides. It is also exhibited in an aggregator's span of practitioner tools, in the forms, indexes, directories, statistical surveys, and public records that bring routine legal instruments and key supporting data together under a single roof.

- **Platforms.** The leading aggregators have sophisticated interfaces and search engines that integrate high-level content and allow it to be searched, printed, saved, and formatted in value-added ways. Again, for the legal researcher, the linchpin is time savings. The aggregators offer the most advanced search syntax on the market, specialized algorithms, a wide array of download and display options in several formats, and an updating schedule that often surpasses official sources when it comes to the digital publication of primary law. In the legal content industry, quantity and quality are obligatory for building a strong and lasting reputation. However, what separates a few from the rest is an infrastructure that permits the content to be extracted and federated with business-amplifying speed and effectiveness.

An aggregator's capacity as a distinct knowledge facilitator comes from its combining of multiple information sources (or relevant parts of them) into new and valuable information packages through the application of computer algorithms and analytics. Portions of desired content are distilled and formatted into reports customized to provide answers for the matter at hand. They are ideal for holistic overviews of subjects that invite numerous interpretations based on jurisdiction (e.g., state surveys of specific topics within general legal areas like public health or insurance) or for amalgamating small yet essential information items that are scattered across separate databases, such as the judicial decisions, transcripts, and scholarly articles involving or authored by experts who offer their testimony to litigants in technical or scientific cases. In addition to saving time, such focused reports can help one to identify major issues and potential red flags.

The power of platform is most fully expressed in the citator (which I briefly discussed in Chapter 2). This is an index that accumulates the primary and secondary sources that cite or refer to a specific case decision, regulation, or statute. Among primary sources, it indicates the cited law's treatment, that is, how the subsequent citing sources have interpreted it. The significance of the treatment depends on the citing source's jurisdiction and its level of authority. Negative treatment can be critical and give one pause before citing a case, or it can overturn and invalidate the piece of legislation one was going to base one's case upon. Positive treatment can be affirming and thereby solidify a precedent's status as "good law." Treatment can also be neutral and simply analyze a previous decision, which might provide additional jurisprudential insight. The list of secondary sources citing one's law can give varying levels of analysis. Any publication that cites the law (in its official citation format) will be retrieved. It might be a passing mention of a single sentence or an entire article or chapter devoted to its detailed exposition. Unfortunately, you will not know until you click on the hyperlinked citing source and open the document.

The two most relied-upon citators for American firm librarians are Shepard's (Lexis) and KeyCite (Westlaw). Shepard's originated in print and grew to become the gold standard of its form. It is now used almost exclusively online. KeyCite, born digital, was Westlaw's attempt to remain competitive against its only real rival, since a powerful citator is a big selling point in the legal marketplace. Perhaps more than any other finding tool, citators are ideal for electronic use. The deeply hyperlinked structure of integrated databases creates an optimal delivery mechanism for rapidly compiling interconnected information. In fact, in print, citators are time-consuming, clunky, and difficult to understand. In digital form, one would be hard-pressed to come up with a more productive legal research aid.

Citators are sometimes described as primarily case law research tools, perhaps because they included only judicial decisions when first published in print. Another reason is that the most critical use of a citator by a firm lawyer is as a reliable indicator of the status of a case. Among common law practitioners, judge-made law represents a ceaseless stream of primary sources to be construed and interrelated. With a mouse click, a citator eliminates much of the onerous interpretive work of determining a case's judicial treatment and the depth of that treatment.

However, Shepard's and KeyCite pull in a plethora of citing references, some of them cases, statutes, and regulations, some of them treatises, handbooks, and review articles. A citator's reach does not extend to every source in an aggregator's repertoire of databases. The algorithm behind it is not that powerful – yet – but it does embrace those online resources most useful to an informed practice of law.

Currently, the two aggregators that stand apart in terms of quality, quantity, and interface, particularly for American practitioners, are the Westlaw and Lexis platforms. When librarians and lawyers evaluate entrants into the database market or take a trial subscription to a new content product, they inevitably compare the offerings to Westlaw (*http://web2.westlaw.com*) or Lexis[1] (*www. lexis.com*). For good or ill, this pair is the baseline by which other integrated resources are judged.

Westlaw and Lexis have recently introduced new platforms. WestlawNext (*http://store.westlaw.com/ westlawnext/default.aspx*) arrived in early 2010. Lexis Advance (*www.lexisnexis.com/newlexis/advance/*) was rolled out in late 2011.[2] Each is marketed as a "next-generation legal research platform" which uses a new and powerful proprietary search engine behind a completely redesigned interface. Both stress a Google-like search function that simultaneously accesses the aggregators' entire collection of databases. Results can be filtered and displayed according to various facets (e.g., by source or court). The differences between these "next-gen" platforms and their "classic" antecedents are substantial and probably impact every aspect of legal research, not least of all the mechanics of search. The implications have been considered (see Ambrogi, 2011; Wheeler, 2011; Sellers and Gragg, 2012) and no doubt will continue to be. But despite their cutting-edge look, feel, and architecture, the WestlawNext and Lexis Advance platforms are closer to high-level re-iterations of the classic versions than a wholly new type of legal research. Searching may be faster and more intuitive, but they both remain basically the same aggregators with the same content.

If the aggregation market is to be transformed, the prime mover of this change is more likely to be the rise of Bloomberg Law (*http://about.bloomberglaw.com/info/about/*) rather than the initiation of new platforms by the two established players. I touch upon Bloomberg in the next section on competition.

Legal publishing market: consolidation and competition

There are still many providers of premium legal and business content, although these may be independent or niche publishers. In the United States, however, there has been a striking level of consolidation in the industry. Svengalis (2011) describes the situation bluntly:

> Over the past thirty years the legal publishing industry in the United States has been transformed from one comprising more than two dozen competitors of some size and professional reputation into an oligarchy dominated by three international conglomerates: Thomson Reuters, Reed Elsevier and Wolters Kluwer.

Thomson Reuters is the parent company of Westlaw. Reed Elsevier owns LexisNexis. Wolters Kluwer owns Aspen Publishers (*www.aspenpublishers.com*) and Commerce Clearing House (CCH) (*www.cch.com*). These four entities and the other law-related subsidiaries owned by Thomson, Reed, and Wolters control most of the legal publishing market. The global parents are multi-billion-dollar corporations that include many divisions, services, and products, some of which are explicitly law or business related and others which are not but are employed in legal practice, since such practice now operates in an increasingly multi-disciplinary and interconnected world. The databases marketed primarily to law firms also contain sizable amounts of tax, health, accounting, and financial resources. The size and assets of these publicly-traded companies can best be appreciated by looking at the periodic financial reports they make available on their company websites.[3]

A recent entrant to the legal information industry is Bloomberg Law. Bloomberg (*www.bloomberg.com*) is a leading financial media and information services provider familiar to the law and library community mainly from its Bloomberg Professional platform, the so-called Bloomberg terminal, a dual-screened computer workstation providing extensive real-time business news and current and historical debt, equity, and commodity pricing. The company has been assembling a growing amount of primary and secondary law sources, initially contained in its terminal but then offered in a separate Web-based product, Bloomberg Law. In 2011, Bloomberg acquired (for nearly $1 billion) the Bureau of National Affairs (BNA), a highly respected, employee-owned American publisher of legal and tax information (see Bloomberg, 2011).

This incorporation of BNA content, together with enhanced functionality, a dramatic re-design, and a determined marketing campaign, have forced the legal information community to reexamine its competitive landscape. Debate and speculative coverage in the media, both mainstream and library-directed, have been plentiful (see Hodnicki, 2012(a), (b), (c), and (d); Niemeier, 2012; O'Grady, 2012a; Summers, 2011). Much of the discussion revolves around Bloomberg Law's role as a major competitor to Westlaw and Lexis. Central to this status is its capacity to be a primary provider of legal information. Can it become a top-shelf aggregator? That is, does it have the comprehensive resources and functionality – and can it keep building on those resources and improving its functionality – to stand next to Westlaw or Lexis as an equal? Can it even become a sole primary provider, offering enough strength and scope for a law firm to consider dropping Westlaw or Lexis and adopting Bloomberg for its information needs? Several librarians think this is possible. Most are waiting before passing judgment and, above all, before switching over and shedding the industry standards. It is too early to tell whether Bloomberg will garner the subscriber base, widespread brand recognition, and near-encyclopedic resources to become a true equal.

One undisputed result of all this competition is a drive by the major aggregators to continually add to its content availability. Of course, this same push to distinguish themselves in terms of resources also leads to an increased level of industry mergers and acquisitions. To properly control and promote distinctive products, you have to own them outright. One would assume that this nonstop competition would result in price savings for the consumer, but this has not been generally the case, although Bloomberg Law's unique pricing terms might change that. I will discuss some of the pricing issues below. Disproportionate market power held by a handful of players does not create a price-flexible business climate. The subscriptions to major aggregator services by large law firms will likely remain very expensive.

An indirect consequence of an annual rise in subscription prices may be a pressure on vendors to regularly augment the quality and quantity of their offerings. Their prices are high and seem to be getting higher, but vendors can partially justify these increases by demonstrating real improvements in content and functionality. High cost does have this one benefit, although it feels remote and perhaps unpersuasive to the typical institutional subscriber. New topical databases are added, formerly print-only titles are introduced in digital format, and interfaces are noticeably refined. Similarly, the intense competition between the three or four top companies instigates continuous enhancement, which will likely endure simply because the consumer has come to expect it as a natural state of affairs.

Absent successful intervention by antitrust authorities, the leading vendors' exertions to innovate and diversify their products will mean more industry consolidation in the coming years. In regard to doing business with those that control high-quality structured legal knowledge, lawyers and librarians will not have many options to choose from. However, because of the vendor disposition to perpetually update, amend, and upgrade – which fundamentally impacts the use of monetized time – "legal research continues to get easier, quicker, cheaper, more user-friendly" (Jones, 2010). Of course, the "cheaper" part of the quote above is a matter open to dispute.

My observations above, though critical, are not meant to castigate large legal publishers for engaging in practices that are common in an open and free market. I am sure that the economic beliefs that philosophically underpin them are accepted on a basic level by most of this book's readers. Publishers, firm-employed lawyers, and firm librarians all live by the dictates of profit-seeking, competitive enterprise. Indeed, to conspicuously deviate from these conventions might be considered unprofessional and even inexcusable to these very people. Consequently, I have no intention of inserting a politicized edge into my discussion. My comments are designed to point out the features of the legal publishing environment that firm librarians need to be aware of. Chief among them is the industry's oligarchic nature. Some of the practical aspects of a librarian's daily interactions with vendors and suppliers are better handled if this context is appreciated. Two enduring parameters are the industry's pricing policies and the contractual and personalized relationships that librarians and vendors engage in.

Pricing issues

Database subscriptions constitute substantial overhead costs to law firms. Some of this money can be recouped through recovery policies, although not all firms bill back for online research and the ones that do may have varying success in realizing the reimbursement. High prices for premium products and efforts to pass the cost of using them onto clients are not peculiar to the legal information realm. What is distinctive to transactions with the major legal vendors are the variable pricing and access arrangements that stem from a library's contractual agreements. Such agreements are prerequisites to accessing the suppliers' services. Prevailing licensing practices have characteristics worth noting:

- There is an overall lack of transparency for law librarians who seek an understanding of customary licensing terms in their field. Most firms are required to agree to non-disclosure clauses as part of their deals. These legally obligate subscribers to keep the terms of their contracts confidential. Industry peers cannot share their offers or acceptances of pricing plans, discount adjustments, or special exclusions. This information barrier further confounds an area already hard to navigate because of its overly legalistic wording and definitional opacity.

- Non-disclosure provisions only aggravate the suspicions legal professionals hold regarding differential pricing deals. Different plans and discounts are held by firms of relatively equal user size and access levels, and some of these differences might be considered unfairly large if they were available for public inspection. The existence of these differences has not been confirmed with hard empirical evidence but all major subscribers in the legal publishing world assume they are commonplace.

Such differential terms follow logically from the real-life contract transactions among organized business enterprises. The negotiations involved in initial subscriptions and subsequent renewals take place at individualized levels, between one or a few representatives on either side. They are often drawn out and contentious. There is a good deal of back-and-forth offers, counter-offers, and delaying tactics. Senior account representatives communicate directly with library managers or directors. If the proceedings stall, the vendor might bring in an even more senior person, who might be met with firm counsel. Both sides engage in their fair share of brinkmanship.

Law firms represent major accounts with reliable streams of revenue. Vendors are highly motivated to sign those firms on as regular customers. A similar give-and-take will commence at renewal time. Some firm representatives are more aggressive and effective in their bargaining, and vendors are willing to budge on various issues to get or retain that client. Therefore, different licensing arrangements will be out there. Firm librarians need to be aware of this disparity, if only to arm themselves with a more grounded understanding of their business surroundings.

- Electronic database vendors are still large publishers of print titles. There are technological and financial challenges to adopting a business model that will adequately balance both products. Vendors face the consequences of their digital accomplishments. Namely, their widespread and effective switch to an online environment has led to customers cancelling many of their hardcopy subscriptions. There are some titles that are maintained in the physical collection as well as accessed electronically because of attorney demand or perceived importance to the firm's needs. However, the general trend has been waves of print cancellations – and subsequent loss of publisher revenue.

One defensive measure embraced by vendors is the restrictive bundling of their products into print and electronic combinations.[4] Subscribers are often compelled to enter into narrow content arrangements where attractive discounts (but still high costs) are offered on the condition they purchase both hardcopy titles and digital access. The combined price is steeper than taking out an all-electronic subscription, but the non-discounted plan of digital-only often seems unreasonably and perhaps punitively high. Another version of bundling is when a vendor packages several databases into a single discounted plan but charges highly for those same databases when subscribed to individually. These aggregated resources can be topically disparate and several can be irrelevant to a firm's needs. However, the vendor's restrictive pricing can make a firm's a la carte approach downright cost-inefficient. Taking one or the other offer, or neither, is dependent on the circumstances of the specific firm. A similar licensing setup is familiar to academic librarians, who refer to it as the "Big Deal" (Frazier, 2001).

An alternative to forcing customers to buy bundled print and digital products is Thomson/West's introduction of Library Maintenance Agreements (LMAs) (*http://store.*

westlaw.com/support/print-pricing-options/library-maintenance-agreement/default.aspx). LMAs are fixed-rate, multi-year contracts incorporating all of a library's West Publishing print titles into a single agreement. Although seen by some as an attempt by the publisher to sustain its future print revenue when many libraries are eliminating their hard copies, it can be a viable option for institutions wishing to keep print costs under control through predictable pricing. Set annual increases are guaranteed. Billing and invoicing are more streamlined and manageable. A Library Maintenance Agreement is cost-effective for a library that has a solid enough grasp of its needs and objectives that it can skillfully plan its collection several years in advance. One pitfall is that once the agreement is signed, the customer is locked into it. This may result in paying for expensive print titles that are no longer used, such as when a practice group weakens or dissolves. The titles can be cancelled and their supplements ceased, but the contracted pricing stays the same. If widely successful, it is conceivable that other major vendors will initiate similar types of plans, albeit under different names.

- Pricing can vary according to whether the firm has enterprise access or a set number of individual password holders. Complete access for all can be gained through IP-authentication of the firm's internet protocol addresses, although sometimes a firm-wide subscription entails giving a user name and password to anyone who requests it rather than seamless authentication. There are no intrinsic cost differences between the two. However, in practice, smaller premium content producers strongly urge or even require subscribers to take out firm-wide contracts. They can generate more revenue from an enterprise plan than by small licenses containing a few users from one or two of the firm's specialized groups. Librarians are painfully aware of the predicament where they are constrained to purchase wide access to a critical niche product for an excessive price based on the total number of attorneys in the firm, but then discover that usage is limited to a handful of practitioners.

The advantage of enterprise access for librarians and lawyers is that it usually comes with flat-fee pricing. That is, once the annual subscription price is paid, all designated users can search, download, and print as much as they desire. There are no additional fees beyond the yearly one-time cost. Users can remain logged on as long as they like. Without the cost and time pressures of hourly and transactional pricing, both focused research and serendipitous discovery are maximized. One drawback to flat fee pricing is a lack of charge-back mechanisms for cost recovery. Some databases, however, are offering the option to enter matter numbers on special screens that time the transactions and maintain detailed usage reports. Smaller vendors favor firm-wide access for its relative administrative ease. It does not cause nearly as much solicitude over compliance issues because there are no restricted passwords that can be shared.

For the two leading legal database providers, Lexis and Westlaw, charging for each search, download, or printing is their preferred business model. They have licensing arrangements with large firms whereby the firms agree to spend a predetermined monthly amount. If the monthly spends are less or more than that amount, the contract calls for certain differential pricing levels to be applied. When renewed, the previous year's usage is evaluated and referred to during negotiations. The problem for most librarians, especially those who have not seen the terms of their firm's contracts, is that the pricing implications of these hefty agreements are difficult to decipher. The formulas for determining how much a search costs if it falls *within* the designated monthly spend are hard enough to figure out. The truly challenging task is being able to relay a clear price to an attorney for transactions that have *exceeded* the monthly amount – particularly when librarians have no idea how much has been charged so far at any given moment.

To many a firm librarian's pleasure, WestlawNext and Lexis Advance have instituted more comprehensible pricing schemes. Each has moved closer to flat-fee pricing at the individual searching and downloading levels. Currently, in Lexis Advance, transactional searching across all the system's databases is free, with a cost being incurred when a document is opened or downloaded. Access charges depend on the source type, with secondary sources and litigation materials (such as court briefs and orders) being more expensive. In WestlawNext there is a single fee for searching and downloading primary law documents, with an additional document download fee attached to secondary sources and litigation materials. These are retail charges and a firm's individualized subscription plan would delineate its discounts from the retail base model.

Although this new structure is an improvement over the multiple pricing schedules in the classic versions of Westlaw and Lexis, it still falls short of what the law firm community really desires: true flat-fee pricing. It wants to pay a fair and single price (monthly or annually) for unlimited access to all content, changing only via contractual negotiation at renewal time. In the absence of this, the community would settle for a manageable set of stable and reasonable pricing options, applied equally across subscribers, and comprehensible to administrators, lawyers, librarians, and clients.

The emergence of Bloomberg Law as a major database contender will likely have discernible impact on the industry's licensing practices. These effects will be seen in the ways vendors handle pricing transparency and predictability. The motivation will be partly a competitive reaction and partly a response to customers (and the clients of customers) that have developed an affinity for a comprehensible and stable costing of digital resources. As evidenced by the subscription model of its financial database, Bloomberg Professional, the company has a reputation for adhering to a single price for all customers.

Niemeier (2012) gives a good overview of Bloomberg Law's consistent pricing. There are two subscription options, one for individual passwords and one for firm-wide access. As of this writing, the first option is $450 per user per month, with small increases every two years. For the second option, initial pricing is determined by the number of US lawyers, with the $450 per user monthly fee being activated by the fifth subscription year. All Bloomberg Law and BNA content are included in both plans. Though there is some ambiguity in the initial pricing language contained in the firm-wide option, the overall transparency and relative simplicity of the schemes are refreshing. At the moment it is difficult to determine how successful Bloomberg has been in garnering firm-wide contracts. It is worth pondering that a much slower customer adoption rate than anticipated might force a turn to more traditionally differential pricing. But there is enough excitement by librarians and attention by industry leaders to forecast significant changes in the ways legal information is accessed and sold. How these changes will transpire and what forms they take are presently unclear.

Vendor relationships: dedicated representatives, training, and demonstrations

Vendor-librarian relationships do not harbor any grave pitfalls, although attentiveness to the interests and influences behind one's professional contacts is always a useful inclination to possess. Firm librarians will interact with numerous vendors. The size of the company and the subscription one's firm has with it will greatly influence the relationship. With a small publisher that produces one or a few resources, vendor contact may be limited to brief communications via a customer service telephone number or email address. Perhaps the librarian will have the name of an actual sales representative but only talk to that person at renewal time or to resolve a sporadic access problem. As one goes up the vendor chain, to the multi-product providers with much larger support and sales staffs, it is more likely one's account will be assigned to a dedicated representative. This person will provide personalized training (or arrange for it) and call in regularly to the firm to see if all is well.

Any sizable company can apply impressive amounts of technological, promotional, and personnel support to distinguish itself from its competitors. However, in terms of market penetration among law firms and law schools, brand recognition, resource portfolio, and sustained staff presence in the field, Westlaw and Lexis occupy a unique perch when it comes to client-vendor relationships in the legal information world.

As one enters into extensive license agreements with these leading database providers, one encounters a distinctive vendor relationship. The major client is deemed preferred and treated accordingly. The librarians and lawyers whose firms maintain these big accounts will be keenly aware of this favored status. They experience the organized resources, ambitions, and expertise that a powerful commercial enterprise directs at them. There is an all-encompassing feel to it. It captivates.

Bright and devoted account representatives sit in the library once a week. For a firm librarian, the front line account representative will be the most recognizable manifestation of the vendor after the product interface itself. Providing friendly and intelligent human assistance is a tenet of excellent customer service but it serves the vendor's business interests as well.

Representatives are effective liaisons with familiar faces, known on a first-name basis. They answer questions, settle issues, and personalize the account. Librarians and representatives often converse as if they were fellow office workers. Account matters are professionally handled but the interactions can be informal and personable. Family events, hobbies, and planned vacations might be talked about. There is a likability and perception of proficiency that help to create a strong bond between client and vendor.

A gracious representative/trainer on site who offers constructive guidance will reinforce the positive connotations a user has for the database. The resource must speak for itself in terms of quality and user-friendliness, but one should not dismiss the ultimate business objectives that are advanced by providing a favorable social and emotional setting for the product experience. Representatives are usually former lawyers or librarians, so their clients can readily identify with them. Their professional credibility is high. When representatives leave a vendor's employment, they frequently pursue work in one of the legal professions.

When firms experience issues their account representative cannot resolve or are not authorized to resolve, such as a major billing dispute, the firms have recourse to higher ranking people in the vendors' organizations. Senior account representatives or regional supervisors can step in to take charge of a client's serious problems. This may involve crediting the client's account for substantial sums of money in the event of erroneous search charges – or affirming corporate policy and offering to compromise on a much lower credit. These senior staffers likely will confer with the library manager, a firm director, or firm counsel. However, librarians are familiar with how readily available the vendors' advanced trouble-shooters are to a distressed client. This "hot line" accessibility signifies that even the vendor's higher operational levels are always there for the client. They are consistently responsive with an answer or a next-level attempt at a solution if the lower level endeavor fails to satisfy. Once you have experienced such an ambient quality of customer service, you get into the habit of seeing it as the only way to go. Any vendor not offering such encompassing service could then be perceived as unacceptably lacking.

The customer service regime of account representatives and senior managers is complemented by an extensive telephone and email reference support system. The helpline is staffed 24 hours a day by the vendors' own experts, who often hold law degrees. Users can call any time and obtain answers to pressing questions about search strategies and content availability.

Personalized and widely attainable instruction by live trainers also gives the impression that a vendor is an entrenched player. It establishes its reputation as the natural choice for all right-thinking information professionals. The power of this sheer presence affects attorneys even before they become attorneys. "This enormous investment in training is made in order to seamlessly ease the law student into seeing Lexis and Westlaw as the reality of legal research." (Berring, 2012) An artful and convivial training session on a platform that can perform an immense array of search and aggregating functions on a dazzling collection of information resources is something that lodges in the consciousness of the legal researcher. There are also plentiful subsequent opportunities for users to explore new resources and analytics through enthusiastic demonstrations and generous trial subscriptions.

The fortifying face-to-face training and demos are augmented with lunch-and-learn get-togethers where librarians are invited to local vendor offices or even hotel conference rooms for sneak peeks at not-yet-formally-rolled-out enhancements or exclusive content additions. These can include catered meals and can be closer to social events than to mere instructional sessions. The vendors' regional library relations representatives are on hand at these sittings. These representatives are savvy client relations people. They possess the requisite sales personalities for reassuring librarian-clients that their unique needs are being addressed.

The machinery of polished corporate communications can be quite impressive. Vendors launch numerous websites, each one aimed at an identifiable user group. They offer focused news stories, commentary by staff writers and guest authors, and product reviews. Indeed, they are often marketed as well-packaged online tools for various communities of practice rather than as collections of useful topical material. Vendors also publish newsletters on law and research-related subjects, training manuals and webinars, white papers, podcasts, and blogs. All are professionally designed and formatted. The visual style and informational substance of these productions reinforce the notion that one is dealing with coordinated and capable outfits who really know their specialties.

Underscoring the social psychological importance of the vendor's personal representatives, its marketing presence, and its field saturation is not meant to insinuate any shady motives to vendors. It is just a fact that a client's total user experience is a material factor in the perceived value of the service. The research tool itself may be the most significant aspect, but it is not the only one.

Ideally, current and future users should recognize that these well-orchestrated training and support endeavors might influence their evaluation and eventual acceptance of the service to the exclusion of other, less financially-backed services. These latter services may be comparable but less costly, or perhaps even superior in some relevant ways.

Of course, even in the absence of the above organized elements, there is the sway of simple inertia. There is the natural human tendency to remain with the situations that have proven reliable in the past. Though subjected to oft-repeated accusations of high cost, the major vendors have successfully fulfilled the basic research needs of librarians and lawyers for a long time. A firm can make the switch to several lower-cost service providers as alternatives, but this entails investing large amounts of time and planning. Cancellations could face possibly insurmountable resistance from users who have made the old products ingrained parts of their work flows. Also, one can foresee user dependence on these vendors increasing with the move to e-books. Such digital products promise a release from desktop-limited research with mobile, truly anywhere access. The vendor that takes advantage of this format will innovate the delivery method of its premium content as well as circulate its brand far beyond the office setting.

Putting all this aside, one also has to admit that perhaps the aggregators are so ensconced and unquestioned in the legal information universe because they give users what they want and are so plainly good at what they do.

Notes

1. Lexis is the dedicated legal research database of the LexisNexis corporation. The company offers many focused products. Its Nexis database (*www.nexis.com*) is marketed as more of a general research product, strong on news and business sources. It contains some legal content but is overshadowed by Lexis in the law firm market.

2. Lexis Advance was first released as Lexis Advance for Solos in 2010 and then re-branded as Lexis Advance for Associates the following year. Now it is officially called Lexis Advance (see Ambrogi, 2011).

3. Their annual and quarterly financial reports can be found at: Thomson Reuters (*http://ir.thomsonreuters.com/phoenix. zhtml?c=76540&p=irol-reportsAnnual*); Reed Elsevier (*www. reedelsevier.com/investorcentre/reports%202007/Pages/ Home.aspx*); and Wolters Kluwer (*www.wolterskluwer.com/ Press/Reports*).

4. Bundling is sometimes referred to as a tying arrangement, which is defined by the Legal Information Institute as "An agreement in which the seller conditions the sale of one product (the 'tying' product) on the buyer's agreement to purchase a separate product (the 'tied' product) from the seller." (*http://www.law.cornell.edu/wex/tying_arrangement*).

Research sources and systems

Abstract: Legal research is the application of a librarian's searching and organizing skills to the world's law-related content. Before these primary and secondary sources are analyzed and determined to be relevant, they have to be obtained. Expert firm librarianship is defined by knowing where valuable content is found as much as by how it can be filtered and applied. It is also a matter of ascertaining the content properties of an information item. Authoritativeness, exclusivity, aggregation, format, context, and currency are among the more defining properties to be aware of. Understanding the locations or conduits of content is significant because these databases and repositories will contain, allow, or afford access to information items with specific properties. Together, the properties and the conduit will influence how, when, and if a source is used. A firm librarian's core conduits are full-service legal platforms; specialized but wide content; free but credible websites; internal firm knowledge; document delivery services; blogs and wikis; and library listservs.

Key words: content; affordance; aggregation; exclusivity; context; conduits; blogs; wikis; listservs

Content properties

A recurring theme in this book has been the basic significance of primary and secondary source content for the practice of law. A firm librarian's essential working material is the tremendous quantities of legal and business resources out there, in multiple formats and with varying levels of accessibility. Content is searched, organized, and assembled through the application of information management skills and competencies. But this material must reach the expert comprehension of librarians before it can be crafted into actionable knowledge. It has to be delivered. The world's profusion of information-bearing items is found somewhere. Delivery is predicated on databases, repositories, and shelves, physical or Web-based. Accomplished firm librarians do not know the exact locations of all the items they seek, but they do know the best places to look for them. They have a cultivated understanding of these conduits of content.

Several properties of content will influence where it is found, if and how it is used, and how costly it will be to access it. Another way of expressing this is to say that "the properties of objects determine the possibilities for action" (Harper and Sellen, 2002). These are sometimes referred to as an object's "affordances." Gaining a confident grasp of how these factors impact judgments of value and how you can effectively navigate them only come through extensive experience in the library field. Some properties to be conscious of include:

- **Authoritativeness.** The value of content is often influenced by how authoritative its producer is – or is perceived to be. Perhaps in the legal world more than anywhere else, who or what created the information is paramount. Its practitioners interpret and act according to structures of established authority. For primary sources such as laws, regulations, and court decisions, the official, original government and judicial sources are authoritative, that is, they are legally binding and controlling. For the secondary sources that explain and apply the primary material (e.g., treatises, journal articles, and commentaries), those with industry-confirmed credentials and reputations possess the most commanding authority. Acceptance of their reasoning can be said to be intellectually rather than legally obligatory. Authoritative primary sources are not necessarily costly to access, since such material is available freely on government websites. What can be expensive are the editorial enhancements that third-party aggregators add to the primary material, making it easier and quicker to search and cross-reference. Authoritative secondary sources, in contrast, are frequently costly to acquire, if only because they are costly to produce and distribute.

- **Language.** International firms function in a globalizing world. Their offices and clients are located in different legal jurisdictions and their transactions are cross-border. The fundamental obstacle for librarians is being able to recognize a foreign jurisdiction's structures of authority, that is, its hierarchy of legal bodies and their methods of publication. What source is controlling? Where can one find its most current authoritative version? In addition to the natural ignorance of any researcher facing a very different legal jurisdiction for the first time, there are the sometimes confounding differences between systems that follow either a common law or a civil legal tradition.

This incomprehension takes on a whole new dimension when the foreign system is in a different language. Secondary sources can be proficiently translated and retain substantial practical value. Primary sources are another matter. Officially sanctioned translations of foreign laws are not common. However, even if translated by a government body, the law is a linguistically nuanced creation. Legislative intent can pivot on the subtle interpretation of a single word. Many terms do not have real equivalents outside of their native languages. Most attorneys will be averse to advising on a consequential transaction based on the translation of a law.

International firms often have staff lawyers who are fluent in the major languages of the business world. Smaller firms do not have such linguistic availability. And sometimes a global firm gets involved in a matter in a geographical location far removed from any of its offices, and where the native language is rarely found in cross-border deals. If a jurisdiction's laws are not found easily in public sources, the official version of those laws in its native language will be a rather exclusive piece of content. If the original is obtained, a fluent expert must be brought in to translate and interpret. The rarity of the language in which a content source is expressed can make that source very costly to properly access and apply to one's matter.

- **Exclusivity.** The inaccessibility of an information source will determine how costly it is to obtain in terms of time, money, and effort. Presumably, the harder an item is to access – because it is rare, scarce, or closely guarded – the more expensive and time-consuming it is to get possession of it. If the searcher lacks resources or time, the item is less likely to be pursued, let alone used. Some content is so exclusive that wealth is meaningless; only connected insiders have access. This could be the case with some analytical reports or privately collected data open only to an industry association's members. Frequently, firm attorneys can get their hands on exclusive company or trade material as a result of their professional affiliations with institutional clients or because they have working relationships with lawyers in other firms who have access themselves. For the librarians in the same firm, however, attaining this documentation without similar connections might be impossible.

- **Format.** The significance of format is often unreasonably discounted by some professionals when asked what they value most in their information sources. However, format is an integral part of the totality of the information package because it affects the time invested in the task at hand, whether it be surveying, comparing, or compiling. A well-designed format facilitates comprehension through the strategic use of size, spacing, and font. Badly formatted material frustrates readers by increasing the amount of time it takes to make sense of the material. It can detract from a presentation's visual appeal and coherency and might give an attorney second thoughts about passing the document onto a client. Often, one's evaluation of a format's strengths and weaknesses is an expression of personal taste. Sometimes there is wide agreement that a source's formatting is among its most impressive aspects – or that it begs for a fundamental re-design. But, whether the reasons behind the appraisal are idiosyncratic or rooted in strong consensus, formatting can impel a librarian or lawyer to use one database over another, particularly if both resources are comparable in other areas.

- **Aggregation.** As discussed in the previous chapter, aggregated premium content sources are powerful assets for the legal information vendors that control them. The strength of aggregation lies in how much and how diverse one's content is and with what levels of functionality and efficiency multiple sources are combined. How complete are the sources? How reliably updated? Accessing authoritative aggregated content can save enormous amounts of time, effort, and cognitive exertion, as there is far less need to constantly shift between information products that could have very different use requirements. As this book has repeatedly affirmed, monetized time is among the law firm community's most valuable commodities. Aggregated high-quality databases can be costly, but accessing the individual resources separately would incur a higher cost in the long run.

- **Context.** A source's usability and reliability increase the more contextual support it receives. Context does not necessarily mean pairing an information item with an explanatory annotation or putting it into theoretical perspective by adding external commentary, although such practices are instances of estimable contextualization. Context is the relational grounding of a piece of information against the source that created it or that maintains its information-bearing identity.

  It can be a government website that digitally posts an official version of its nation's laws. Though not accompanied by secondary source analyses, the manifest structure and backing of the site itself is the key context. It positions the information as being derived from an originating, authoritative source, thereby confirming its legitimacy. In a similar manner, the varied database items contained in aggregate form in Lexis or Westlaw are presumed to be what the vendors claim them to be – current, authentic, and authoritative – because both these knowledge platforms are widely accepted by users to be legitimating contexts. That is, if Westlaw or Lexis has them, they must be trustworthy. The traditions, reputations, and proven experience that imbue these brands are persuasive enough. Such a sterling context commands premium prices. On the other hand, many websites on the Internet have no context whatsoever. Their server affiliations are obscure and they are apparently unrelated to any recognizable source. Such sites are freely accessed, but without context they should be used only in limited ways and with great caution.

- **Currency.** This is the property of being updated to accurately reflect changes in the environment or the world at large. Only current law is "good" law, so the imperative of keeping current in legal practice is self-evident. For the tracking of legal and regulatory developments, whether it is the actual decisions of lawmakers or the context-endowing news coverage that readily follows them, currency is something for which researchers will pay a handsome price. Granted, a substantial amount of reliably current information is found on the open Web. However, attorneys and firm librarians realize the high-stakes nature of their profession and turn to the high-cost but valuably contextualized database aggregators for both comprehensiveness and currency.

It should be emphasized that in legal practice, finding "good" current law is not always the goal. Often one needs to determine the *relevant* law that applies in a social or business context. If the event or action in question occurred in the past, then the relevant, applicable law is the statute or regulation that was in effect at the time of the occurrence. If something happened on the first of June in 2000, unless the law addressing the relevant issues and facts remains active on the books in exactly the same form, that old law must be found. If it has been amended at all since the original event, then a version of the law incorporating any changes as of yesterday will not be useful. No other information item other than an older, archived copy of the law as of June 1, 2000 is acceptable.

Systems, databases, providers, and facilitators: the conduits of content

The following is a list of specific locations for primary and secondary source legal and business content. It is not meant to be exhaustive, only to delineate the many channels a firm librarian becomes conversant with when pursuing relevant information. With the possible exception of full-service legal platforms, not all examples within a conduit type will share the same quantity and quality of properties. One only has to look at the Internet to realize this. Many free sites are questionable if not worthless as conduits of knowledge-supporting content. Others, such as those sponsored by universities or governmental agencies, can be among the most authoritative sources of its kind.

Full-service legal platforms

Westlaw and Lexis are the best examples of this kind of conduit. Bloomberg Law is a close competitor. They possess a distinct kind of authority, that of an expert knowledge organization with the skills, technology, and reputation for combining authoritative primary and secondary sources. Their material is varied and comprehensive. In their citators (i.e., KeyCite for Westlaw and Shepard's for Lexis) they offer a contextualizing tool of unparalleled utility. Indexing, editorial enhancements, and value-added analytics are substantial. Cost is high but so are their levels of aggregation and authoritativeness. Choice of formats is extensive. With reliably updated sources and the systematic alerting services to push that content out to users on a rapid and continual basis, currency is among their strongest points. Westlaw and Lexis are also growing their collections of archived statutory and regulatory material. Both have older state and federal laws going back several years. Additionally, they offer some foreign language primary materials, although most of the world's legislation is well out of their reach.

Specialized but wide content

These are large databases that include sizable amounts of primary and secondary sources in several topics as well as some subject-specific news, alerting, editorial features, and finding tools such as indexes. They can be aggregators but they cannot compete with the one-stop shopping of Westlaw or Lexis. Also, they or their corporate parents can be among the bigger participants in the legal or business information market. CCH IntelliConnect is an example. It offers the laws, regulations, and analytical material from its leading tax, securities, labor, and banking reporters and treatises in an integrated, practitioner-focused database. Its resources are valuably contextualized and authoritative. Many of its resources are not necessarily exclusive in the true sense of the word; its primary content is found in other databases and there are often comparable secondary sources by competing publishers. Another example is Hein Online (*http://home. heinonline.org/*), which specializes in classic legal treatises, historical collections of governmental documents, US federal legislative histories, and law journal runs that extend back to their first issues (all in scanned pdf images of the originals).

Like the full-service Lexis and Westlaw, the exclusivity of this conduit type is found in the distinct combination of its primary and secondary sources and the proprietary platform that aggregates and formats them in user-preferred ways. One can argue that Bloomberg Law still resides in this "specialized but wide content" category. Its competitive potential is considerable yet it is not quite a full-service legal platform in the same way Westlaw and Lexis are.

Niche content

This is narrowly specialized content related to one or a few topics and forms. Sometimes it is a platform for the digital versions of print titles found nowhere else. It can also be unique, Internet-only content that practitioners in certain areas have come to perceive as critically authoritative. The publishers employ some combination of veteran journalists, skilled editors, and subject specialists to provide must-have news reporting and in-depth analysis. Niche content's coverage of breaking industry developments makes it one of the most time-sensitive services available. Because of its specialized material, it can be priced steeply. Its combining of subject experts gives it possession of exclusive resources. Law360 (*www.law360.com/*) or the US operation of the Practical Law Company (*http://us.practicallaw.com/*) are examples.

Free but valuable

These are freely available websites, sponsored by reputable governmental entities, educational institutions, or trade associations, that contain authoritative and contextualized primary or secondary sources. Currency, exclusivity, and format can vary. Their main weakness is a lack of aggregating power. Content is dispersed on the site and relevant items are not easily retrieved in a single query. "If a search is performed and the first 10 hits are all irrelevant, confidence is lost" (Ard, 2010). Such free websites are usually powered by weak search engines.

These conduits are best suited for the retrieval of single exclusive or authoritative known-items, such as officially authenticated laws or government documents. For the former, an excellent source is Congress.gov (*www.congress.gov*), the US Library of Congress site for federal legislative resources such as bills, laws, resolutions, and committee reports. It is indispensable for finding recent congressional actions and the status of pending legislation.

An example of a site for valuable policy analysis is the UK
Parliament's Research briefings page (*http://www.parliament.
uk/business/publications/research/briefing-papers/*),
"produced by the Libraries of the House of Commons and
House of Lords and the Parliamentary Office of Science and
Technology (POST)." The US Congressional Research
Service publishes similarly objective and expert analyses of
legal, political, and economic issues; however there is no
single, officially-backed repository for these. They are made
available on various educational, research, and non-profit
websites, e.g. Open CRS (*https://opencrs.com/*) and the
UNT (University of North Texas) Digital Library (*http://
digital.library.unt.edu/explore/collections/CRSR/browse/*).
Some of the best known examples of free but valuable
primary content are the open access legal information
institutes such as Cornell University Law School's pioneering
Legal Information Institute (*http://www.law.cornell.edu/*),
Canada's CanLII (*http://www.canlii.org/en/*), the Australasian
Legal Information Institute (*http://www.austlii.edu.au/*), and
the British and Irish Legal Information Institute (*http://www.
bailii.org/*). The enormous content of fourteen such national
and regional institutes can be browsed or searched
simultaneously at the World Legal Information Institute
(*http://www.worldlii.org/*).

Internal know-how

The memos, practice guides, and templates organized on a
firm's knowledge management systems are among the most
exclusive and contextualized sources a librarian can find. It
is internally produced expertise by the attorneys in one's
own organization and is often customized for a specific set
of legal or business circumstances. The content's author is
usually identifiable and can be directly contacted and

consulted if still employed at the firm. Since much of the material is produced for a client matter, it is confidential. Commonly, internal document databases are open to enterprise search engines and so their content can be aggregated to a certain extent, although downloading, saving, and formatting options are limited. Also, retrieved documents can be batched together, but any discrete content they hold likely cannot be extracted and combined in value-added ways through automated means. Moreover, one would not seek out such internal content for keeping apprised of current legal or business developments.

Document delivery

These are the information resources purchased from external content providers, usually commercial vendors specializing in retrieving third-party publications such as journal articles, technical reports, and archived legislation in print. Public and university libraries also provide such delivery services. The items sought can be difficult to acquire elsewhere, especially in a reasonable amount of time. Since they are isolated resources, accessed intermittently for a prescribed purpose, their properties of timeliness, aggregation, and format are not relevant. They are contextualized by the reputation of the document providers that administer them as well as by already being an integral component of a larger authoritative context, such as the scholarly article or book chapter receiving its credibility from the broader publication of which it is a part. Examples of these providers are the British Library's Document Supply Services (*http://www.bl. uk/reshelp/atyourdesk/docsupply/searchandorderadocument/ index.html*) and the Michigan Information Transfer Source (MITS) at the University of Michigan (*http://www.lib.umich. edu/mits/index.html*).

Blogs and wikis

Any casual web surfer will know that the quality of blogs and wikis on the open Web varies dramatically. However, the sites the everyday searcher visits regularly and perceives as a solid source of information may not satisfy the librarian's content standards. The firm librarian will visit a select group of blogs for breaking news and analytical insights. These are usually affiliated with law firms or other reputable institutions or authored by individuals deemed reliable by those in the field. Law librarians are particularly fond of the difficult-to-find case decisions and government documents frequently posted by credible bloggers. Wikis can offer informative overviews, definitions, and perhaps most useful of all, external links to primary sources. A firm librarian will never forward a wiki entry to an attorney, unless it is the only resource one can discover on a topic and it comes from a highly credible source, such as a university-based wiki. More often than not, wikis are where one would forage for suggestions of search terms to use in more reliable sources, for example, in journal articles or legal encyclopedias.

The opinions and perspectives in law-related blogs can be reliably contextualized if their authors or sponsoring sites are credible. The primary documents posted on them can also be temporarily exclusive if the blog makes them available before anyone else does. However, their formatting and aggregating properties are nearly non-existent. Blogs, no matter how respected and in-the-know their authors may be, are almost never relied upon to the exclusion of other, more established secondary sources. They are supplementing resources that flesh out one's perspectives. As such, authoritativeness is not one of the properties by which they are properly judged.

Library listservs

Firm librarians are voracious users of practice-relevant distribution lists. The most active listservs are sponsored by professional library associations or their specialized divisions. Legal and library news is disseminated widely and rapidly, informative discussion threads on controversial issues are tracked, and training and employment opportunities are advertised. Perhaps the most valuable features of listservs for librarians are the tips, product reviews, and best practices promulgated by highly competent peers. A firm librarian encounters a database problem or seeks an esoteric knowledge source and sends a query to the list. A listserv subscriber somewhere has firsthand experience with the situation and provides guidance. Vendor evaluations are exchanged. The librarians attached to the list may offer to delve into their collections for anyone pursuing an elusive article or treatise section, thereby giving the list the quality of a document delivery conduit.

The library listserv can be the source of current news but propagating timely information is not among its chief functions. Similarly, it possesses no aggregating or formatting properties. Its context and authoritativeness can be assessed by its legitimacy as an advisory or referral service rather than by any content it provides. The list is better understood as a conduit to other types of conduits.

Conclusion:
Law firm librarianship: a
dynamic profession

Abstract: Law firm librarianship is impacted by the professional environments in which it is an established participant: the law firm culture, the legal publishing industry, and general librarianship. Its directions and identity are also impacted by the profound technology-based transformations in the information professions and in society at large. The digitization of ever more information items and the immediate Web-based accessibility of those items create new and heavy expectations from all users. The shape of firm librarianship's future will be determined by these changes and the profession's readiness to confront them. The Googlization of search and the rise of e-books are a few of the more conspicuous trends to be watched. However, firm librarians can best counter any intimations of disintermediation or obsolescence by responding effectively to the two defining qualities of law firm practice: the monetization of time and the contextualized complexity of legal knowledge.

Key words: e-books, corporate law firms, handhelds, mobile devices, technological innovation, Googlization, Dewey & LeBoeuf, economic downturn, disintermediation

The technological, occupational, and economic environments of law firm librarianship have been in a state of flux for several years. The profession's responses to these changes – usually creative and at times reactive – have shaped its contemporary identity. In fields driven by the intersection of technology and knowledge, change is always on their practitioners' minds. But the magnitude of change in such fields seems to have acquired an exponential quality with each passing year. Recent events portend more and larger transformations in shorter spans of time.

As this book has argued, firm librarianship is impacted by several factors. Among the more powerful are: the law firm culture that surrounds it and imposes its own demanding notion of value; the expectations of its users, who carry the diverse and constraining presumptions of both legal professionals and free market consumers; an oligarchic publishing industry that controls the content it depends upon; and an information technology that infuses all of the above with a permeating sense of urgency and transience.

A few events and situations are worth mentioning because they typify the professional issues with which firm librarians are preoccupied.

The law firm world

In 2012, the international law firm of Dewey & LeBoeuf collapsed and filed for bankruptcy. The reasons behind the firm's failure have been discussed elsewhere (see Ax and Prasad, 2012; Ho, 2012; Simmons, 2012; and Stewart, 2012) and will not be analyzed here. Industry observers claimed the firm's problems were apparent for some time. However, the speed and drama with which the breakdown unfolded and the major media attention it generated from both the legal press and mainstream publishers made the crash rife with implication. The dominant motif seemed to be that "Big Law" (that is, global corporate law firms) was on its last legs and needed to make drastic changes to its ways of doing business if it wanted to survive. The Dewey dissolution was interpreted by many as a wake-up call to law firms to reevaluate their business models, ambitions, and staffing structures.

No doubt the anxieties that came to the fore with Dewey had been building in the years since the world financial crisis of 2007 and its subsequent recession. The stunning economic downturn caused large firms to lay off unprecedented numbers of attorneys and support staff (Glater, 2008; Jones, 2009; Dilloff, 2011). Cost cutting and fiscal discipline became norms. The facts of financial adversity were real enough, but the cultural perceptions of hardship and austerity played as much a role in interpreting the firm environment as the facts. Despite having had a fairly unique set of causative factors, the Dewey & LeBoeuf implosion was seen as the embodiment of Big Law inflexibility and dysfunction in the face of a rapidly changing world.

Through sheer proximity to such a tempestuous course of events, firm librarians felt compelled to engage in the same soul-searching as other vested firm professionals. For them, this took the familiar form of a more earnest acceptance of value-creation for their organizations. Librarians have no weight in the determination of fee structures or practice group realignments. They are not participants in high-level strategic planning. But they can re-dedicate their departments to the integrity of their firms' bottom lines. Confronted by budget cutting and the specter of outsourcing, they have taken on more responsibilities, embedded themselves into deeper levels of service commitment, and embraced perpetual self-marketing as a necessary condition of employment. In professional service firms, a higher standard of performance is expected to be sustained once it has been demonstrated to management's satisfaction. Consequently, this striving of firm librarians to confirm their value is not going to diminish any time soon.

User expectations in a high-tech world

A firm library's users will expect the same levels of immediate, anywhere, and convenient access they experience in their personal lives (or in their roles as university students they might have lived not long ago). Communication devices and platforms such as smart phones, tablets, and social networking sites are ubiquitous. Living in a handheld consumer society leads to an expectation of fully mobile connectedness to one's workflow as well as to the private sectors in one's life. Similarly, the exciting rise in e-book consumption has made the general population accustomed to obtaining portable electronic satisfaction for their reading and knowledge needs (Aptara and Publishers Weekly, 2012; Davenport, 2012; O'Brien, Gasser, and Palfrey, 2012).

This assumption is probably most pronounced in younger information consumers, the so-called digital natives, who are born into this unparalleled accessibility as if it were an unobtrusive background.

Firm librarians are well aware of their duty to manage their users' expectations, especially in regard to the technology that determines how and when valuable content is accessed. One challenge comes from the generational differences between many firm librarians, who tend to be older, and the bulk of their users, the younger associates who perform most of the legal research. The age cohort for this latter group remains relatively constant; the firm librarians, if stable with the company, grow older. Today, many firm librarians can probably relate to Ambrogi's (2012) observation:

> It seems quaint now to remember that, in 1995, few lawyers used email or even knew what it was. Back

then, we still preferred the telephone and fax machine. Neither Westlaw nor Lexis-Nexis were accessible through Internet. You still needed to use a dial-up terminal or hard-copy books in the library.

It is equally likely that few starting associates, not to mention law school students, can imagine such an antiquated time.

The buzz around e-books in the firm library community is a reaction to the major legal vendors' incipient yet ambitious move into that territory. Some are announcing partnerships with third-party platform and content providers where the legal suppliers' standard titles will be combined with external scholarly resources to form an e-book super showcase (LexisNexis, 2012). The vendors are making an aggressive push toward widespread use of this digital content, but their marketing and sales rhetoric currently outstrip the everyday realities. There are different technical standards behind the platforms. Concurrent use of two or more e-book purveyors thereby becomes problematic. Conceptions of ownership versus access are murky. Licensing terms are difficult to comprehend. There is also the paramount issue of price. Librarians are skeptical of the vendors' costing logic. Supposedly an e-book is more expensive to initially produce than its print counterpart, but one assumes it will eventually cost far less the more time that digital copy is in existence. But will the e-book be fairly priced after its initial costs are recouped, or will publishers maintain the high cost as a way to keep their overall profits intact?

How successfully the thorny pricing, licensing, and access issues intrinsic to e-books are resolved will set the stage for firm librarians' confrontations with future trends in digital information creation and acquisition.

The simplification of search

Although the legal content industry is always newsworthy for its competition-fueled mergers and consolidations, firm librarians have been more caught up over the ramifications of three new platforms, Bloomberg Law, WestlawNext, and Lexis Advance. Impassioned discussion swirls around the question of whether these "next-generation" research systems afford superior knowledge-generating experiences or if they are just new and quicker ways to perform the same old tasks. Their look and feel are qualitatively different. Information can be visualized in novel ways. But it is too soon to say whether such platforms will be judged to be manifestly better knowledge tools in the hands of already sophisticated searchers. Such an assessment awaits the user conversance that comes from prolonged daily exploration of these products, in addition to the vendors' inevitable upgrades and revisions.

There is also the dispute over whether Bloomberg can become a true peer to the other two. Some presently treat them as equals; others believe they will be in a few years. Either way, the oligarchy will increase by one, if it has not already.

The central selling points of these new platforms are simplified Google-like search boxes and intuitive interfaces and results displays. The introduction of a "single simple query searches everything" approach means a lower barrier to entry for those users who were formerly intimidated by complex queries and granular field searching. The faceted listing of all material rated as relevant (by the system) panders to the hopes of those who look eagerly for the coming of the "unified information environment, that is, an environment where all information can be discovered and accessed using common search methods" (Webster, 2008).

The vendors anticipate that many of these newly added users will be attorneys. This newly born simplicity, which cloaks an equally novel but complex powerhouse algorithm, will presumably allow many more people to do their own information work. However, I do not sense much trepidation among firm librarians that lawyers' will begin to pass them over in favor of a database's shiny new attributes, no matter how arresting its graphics are or how much power it has under the hood.

Predictions for possible directions

In light of the events and trends above, I want to offer a few predictions regarding the possible directions of law firm librarianship:

- Accessing information through digital handhelds is becoming commonplace. Although much of this use now involves fiction and general interest reading, the range of sources available for viewing will significantly broaden. This expansion will include a large amount of legal content. Law and business related news, already a staple of handheld consumption, is ideal for 24/7 mobile access. It is always developing, updating, and "breaking;" its word count is low enough to be comfortably digested on a smaller screen; and it is time-sensitive by definition.

  The migration of more practitioner-based legal items such as treatises and manuals will increase. The screen and keyboard size of mobile devices present some obstacles to sophisticated research, but presumably many handheld interactions are done on-the-go, while commuting, conferring in a courtroom, or meeting with clients at their offices. Sustained, in-depth queries will still be completed on the standard desktop or laptop. However, this may indeed change, in consideration of the sociological reality that people readily adapt to the physical and psychological properties of new media forms. It is conceivable that design innovations, improved delivery mechanisms, and user acclimation will lead to more advanced levels of information handling being performed on handhelds.

Firm librarians who currently use mobile devices to complement their knowledge tool kits appreciate how problematic it would be to carry out thorough and intricate research on such devices. Back at the library they have fast, stable network connectivity; wide, visually inviting computer screens; a generously proportioned workspace where reference documents are within an arm's reach; and at least some remnants of a print collection which, no matter how streamlined it is, perfectly rounds out the research enterprise. Such a setting is uniquely conducive to analytical, exploratory, and multi-tasked information work. I cannot imagine a handheld that can rival such a set of affordances.

While protracted research will prove difficult on handhelds for the foreseeable future, I believe the production of law-related e-books will dramatically increase. This is a natural outcome of the electronic book format's popularity among public library users and consumers in general. The larger legal information vendors are actively moving into this market. As I indicated above, there are unresolved issues of platform compatibility, pricing, and access vs. ownership. Firm librarians are proceeding with caution, but eventually these issues will be worked out. Law firms are too valuable a customer base to lose. Vendor differences over technical standards will cede to compromise. The disconcerting gray pricing will give way to a business model workable for both buyers and suppliers. The well-worn dilemmas, however, will remain. Lawyers will blend e-books into their professional information practices and come to expect them as givens. This perception of indispensability will become the norm as more attorneys are born into a culture where the word "book" summons a digital image as frequently as it does a paper-based one. Sensing the vulnerability of such a captive audience and the chance to bolster revenue, publishers will keep costs high. Also, since the death of the traditional book seems to be more alleged than confirmed, the print-electronic bundling conundrum will persist to some extent. But, even with these formidable challenges ahead, I predict e-books will soon become a very major part of the legal information universe.

- Technological innovation in the creation and use of information has occurred so rapidly and diffusely that it has taken on a self-perpetuating momentum. For lawyers and librarians, as for most people, these tectonic changes have been exemplified in the breathless range of open Web content and the immediate communications of social media. However, now there is a shorter path from the transformative to the mundane. Expectations of plenty are surpassed only by expectations that it all can be had with minimal effort. Everyone has gotten used to the sheer number of information sources retrievable at any time with a few key words typed into a search engine. This has led to what is sometimes referred to as the Googlization of information work. It is the assumption that knowledge discovery happens after one submits a brief, unstructured query to a database and then promptly receives an on-point answer. The database, no matter how sophisticated, need not be understood, let alone mastered. The vendor will have designed and programmed the product with such usability and processing potentiality that no search language has to be learned or basic instructions read through. The connection between relevant information item and its seeker will be seamless and effortless. The question will be parsed into descriptive words and "Googled." No intermediaries or time-consuming structured search strategies are called for. Just plug in the terms and click.

Many people see the Googlization of information work as a holy grail to be sought after. They perceive it as not only tenable but something offering mainly beneficence upon its attainment. After all, such simplicity and convenience are what the market rewards. Librarians and others in the know about how information is created, structured, and found tend to be more skeptical. Such experts have their sights set at more realistic levels. Like Webster (2008), they pursue approximations of the "unified information environment," without going to the extremes of one-click, discernment-free knowledge access.

For law librarians, the next-generation platforms of WestlawNext and Lexis Advance signify the legal market's recognition of general society's ardor for Google-like information consumption. These platforms are explicitly marketed as streamlined search interfaces, backed by unseen yet powerful algorithms. They free users of the cognitive burdens of having to gauge the applicability of narrow (yet on-target) databases or to craft granular field searches. Enter your search terms and the system will display your answer – or a listing of results the algorithm decides are the most relevant. The results will be faceted according to source type and jurisdiction. But your answer is there. It must be. Trust the algorithm. No need to know how it works (it is proprietary anyway). Just trust it.

The vendors have embraced this simplicity to attract and retain younger generations who are being raised on the notion of instant and unmediated knowledge gathering. Moreover, the next generation platforms, reflecting the innovative, resource-rich, and competitive nature of their creator companies, will continuously evolve to incorporate more content and organize it in novel, value-added ways. The combination of palpable ease of use with outstanding content is a persuasive offering for unrefined searchers who seek the potential bounty of information aggregation but lack the skills or patience to adequately confront it with tightly woven search logic. The broad expectations for this type of searching are out there. The suppliers are simply responding to them from a business perspective.

Many firm librarians will see the "one box searches everything" method as extraneous, if not as a step in the direction of overkill. Having a database return all relevant hits from all possible sources may occasionally yield a serendipitous nugget; however, lawyers rarely need to adopt this all-inclusive A-Z approach. They have complex knowledge requirements that call for many different kinds of information – at different times. Their very complexity necessitates that they often be addressed separately. Sometimes a few of the information strands will be retrieved in tandem or together for cross-referencing and comparison. But amassing everything even marginally relevant in a single, wrapped-together search returns a clutter of results. Getting a fix on the truly relevant would then demand more time and cognitive effort. Even a comprehensive query, if it is to be professionally performed, is planned and selective. Certainly, it need not dive feet first into a platform's vast ocean of resources.

Most attorney requests are for a specific – often a *very specific* – content type. For example, if they are looking for a company report with detailed financials such as annual revenues and profits, they are not interested in primary sources like statutes. If they seek precedents of a specific type of court filing from a particular jurisdiction, then news databases will be superfluous sources to include in one's search.

Although heavily promoting their simplified searching features, Lexis and Westlaw do allow some sophisticated queries in their new products. Limited field searching exists and there is an option to choose specific sources to search individually. But granular information seeking in the next-gen platforms currently appears undeveloped if one compares it to the search versatility of the original platforms.

It remains to be seen whether future marketplace entrants will overemphasize the Google-like features their products may have. Over time, I see the WestlawNext and Lexis Advance platforms adopting more advanced search features comparable to their classic antecedents. Once the systems are more firmly grounded in the legal information landscape, the vendors will add a lot more search refinement to the ever-growing content. After all, the technological sophistication of these new systems can easily embrace the entire spectrum of searching, from beginner to expert. They harbor too much knowledge-generating potential to exclude advanced query-building. Consequently, it is only a matter of time before the vendors re-dedicate their enhancement efforts for the benefit of their power searchers.

Librarians will grow to like (even love, I dare say) the new platforms, partly out of necessity when the older ones are retired, and partly due to a steady recognition that the new ones do indeed offer highly useful functions and features. Necessity will be imposed through the not-too-distant retirement of the Westlaw and Lexis legacy systems (the "classic" versions). This will probably be due to the high cost and overall inefficiency of maintaining two major systems with mostly overlapping content. The recognition of value will accrue naturally, as librarians realize that, with time to mature, the new integrated systems are remarkably practicable instruments capable of precise feats of information discovery. Then the disappearance of the classic platforms will not be seen so much as a lamentable "end of an era" but as a routine place marker on the timeline of digital knowledge innovation.

I do not think the vendors' push toward overly simple searching of their legal content will lead to any unsettling issues of librarian disintermediation, let alone of obsolescence. Despite the temptation to embrace the well-marketed logic of next-generation platforms, legal professionals are well aware of the complex nature of their information work. It is rife with interpretative demands and cognitive challenges. At some point, whether it be search, assessment, or utilization, the Google-like interface becomes an impediment to the direct confrontation of relevant information. Someone has to meet reality without a mediating and simplifying overlay. Lawyers know their librarians are there to make that express contact and use their finely honed expertise to deliver the on-point information pearl. And when librarians take on research requests, they "own" those requests and often feel like it is a personal failing if they do not retrieve the answer – even if they are convinced that there is no answer. Google-like simplification is a good option to have, as long as it is not the only option, for it is a pale alternative to the librarian's personalized treatment and mindfulness. Championing such simplification to the neglect of more exacting, cultivated, and *realistic* methods is a descent towards obscuring the true nature of knowledge engagement.

Dynamic and resilient

Librarians have been assailing themselves with thoughts of disintermediation and eventual obsolescence since the emergence of computerized information. Strenuous environmental flux often provokes such radical self-questioning and ambivalence. However, techno-idealism and the advocacy of ever-more automated processes are constant trends in the information professions. The practice of law can be as enamored of its technology-propelled efficiencies as any other knowledge enterprise. Yet, no matter how re-iterated and refined, one's rational procedures can be meaningless if they are not instituted with clear evaluative frameworks in mind. As O'Grady (2012b) insists, "We are constantly driving change into a community of lawyers where there is no universal consensus of what (product technology, platform, interface) is truly intuitive and which is 'not worth the effort.'"

Firm librarianship will remain a dynamic and resilient profession as long as it responds effectively to two defining qualities of law firm practice: the monetization of time and the contextualized complexity of legal knowledge.

The billable hour and monetized time have been cited frequently in this book. A lawyer's time is devoted to resolving consequential legal and business issues, so it is quite expensive. If used inefficiently, it will be costly to the client. If underused, it will be costly to the firm. Obviously, such time is a highly valuable commodity. A firm's financial health is judged by the time its attorneys successfully bill to its clients.

Firm librarians allow attorneys to devote a maximum amount of their time to the expert legal counsel that clients expect. They do this by spending their lesser-valued time searching, organizing, and extracting complex, practice-oriented knowledge. Legal information is fundamentally relational. It is embedded in other, larger, interrelated systems. It is thick, intellectually viscous, and time-consuming. A librarian "simultaneously *expands* and *narrows* the available content that is required by an end user by distilling the most useful content from the broadest number of information sources" (Holden, 2010; emphasis in original). Extricating relevant information items requires the time lawyers cannot spare and the experience and aptitude they do not necessarily possess. They might be able to perform these knowledge tasks on their own, but that is not what they are paid to do. They expertly advise based on the material found, vetted, and presented by librarians.

The law firm librarian's key role is facilitating the practice and business of law by letting lawyers be lawyers. There is something unavoidably human and holistic in such a relationship. I doubt it can be replicated any time soon by a process improvement or a better coded algorithm.

References

Abram, S. (2007) "Web 2.0, Library 2.0 and Librarian 2.0: Preparing for the 2.0 World." Online International Conference, December 4, 2007. Available at: *http://stephens lighthouse.com/files/OnlineIntrenationalProceedings 1.pdf*

Abramovitz, L. (2007) "Life as a Solo Librarian: Master of My Domain." *Law Library Lights* (Newsletter of the Law Librarians Society of Washington D.C.), 50 (2): 19–20. Available at: *http://www.llsdc.org/attachments/wysiwyg/ 232/Lights%20W2007.pdf*.

Adams, C. (2012). "Law Firm Librarians: Out of Sight, Out of Mind." 3 Geeks and a Law Blog, January 10, 2012. Available at: *http://www.geeklawblog.com/2012/01/law-firm-librarians-out-of-sight-out-of.html*.

Agrawal, A. (2012). "In Conversation: Sanjay Kamlani and David Perla, co-CEO's of Pangea3." *Bar & Bench*, June 27, 2012. Available at: *http://barandbench.com/ brief/4/2540/in-conversation-sanjay-kamlani-and-david-perla-co-ceos-of-pangea3*.

Ambrogi, R.J. (2011). "Lexis Launches Advance, its Next-Generation Research Platform." LawSites, December 5, 2011. Available at: *http://www.lawsitesblog.com/2011/12/ lexis-launches-advance-its-next-generation-research-platform.html*.

Ambrogi, R. (2012). "For Legal Professionals, the Internet Has Come a Long Way, But Still Has a Long Way to Go." *LawSites*, February 29, 2012. Available at: *http://www.lawsitesblog.com/2012/02/for-legal-professionals-the-internet-has-come-a-long-way-but-still-has-a-long-way-to-go.html*.

American Association of Law Libraries (2011) *The AALL Biennial Salary Survey & Organizational Characteristics*. Chicago: American Association of Law Libraries.

American Lawyer (2012). 2011 Gross Revenue. Am Law 100. May 2012 issue.

American Lawyer (2011). Most Revenue. The Global 100. October 2011 issue.

Annoyed Librarian (2011) "Public Library Privilege." Library Journal blog, March 16, 2011. Available at: *http://blog.libraryjournal.com/annoyedlibrarian/2011/03/16/public-library-privilege/*.

Aptara and Publishers Weekly (2012). *Revealing the Business of eBooks: The Fourth Annual eBook Survey of Publishers*. Available at: *http://ww3.aptaracorp.com/lp/landingpages/4thebooksurveyregister.html*. (Free registration required.)

Ard, C. (2010). "Legal Research in the Age of Open Law." *Online*, 34:5, 29–32.

Areeda, P.E. and Hovenkamp, H. (2006). *Antitrust Law: An Analysis of Antitrust Principles and Their Application, 3rd ed*. New York: Aspen Publishers/Wolters Kluwer Law & Business.

Association of College and Research Libraries. (2010). *The Value of Academic Libraries: A Comprehensive Research Review and Report*. Researched by Megan Oakleaf. Chicago: Association of College and Research Libraries. Available at: *http://www.ala.org/ala/mgrps/divs/acrl/issues/value/val_report.pdf*.

Association of Research Libraries (2002). *Collections & Access for the 21st-Century Scholar: Changing Roles of Research Libraries*. A Report from the ARL Collections & Access Issues Task Force. ARL, no. 225 (December 2002). Available at: *http://www.arl.org/bm~doc/main.pdf*.

Ax, J. and Prasad, S. (2012). "Dewey Files for Chapter 11 in Record Law Firm Collapse." *Reuters*, May 29, 2012. Available at: *http://www.reuters.com/assets/print?aid=US BRE84S01R20120529*.

Balotti, R.F. and Finkelstein, J.A. (2012). *The Delaware Law of Corporations & Business Organizations, 3rd ed.* New York: Aspen Publishers/Wolters Kluwer Law & Business.

Bates, M.E. (2009) "Do I Look Like a Librarian?" *Online: Exploring Technology & Resources for Information Professionals*, 33 (5): 64.

Berring, R.. (2007) "A Brief History of Law Librarianship." In Balleste, R., Luna-Lamas, S, and Smith-Butler, L. (eds), *Law Librarianship in the Twenty-First Century*. Lanham, Maryland: Scarecrow Press.

Berring, R. "Bloomberg Law: The Wheel Turns." Slaw, May 2, 2012. Available at: *http://www.slaw.ca/2012/05/02/ bloomberg-law-the-wheel-turns/*.

Bird, R. (2012) "Professional Associations and Why They Matter." Slaw, January 20, 2012. Available at: *http:// www.slaw.ca/2012/01/20/professional-associations-and- why-they-matter/*.

Bloomberg L.P. (2011). "Bloomberg Completes Acquisition of BNA." Bloomberg press release, September, 30, 2011. Available at: *http://www.bloomberg.com/news/2011-09- 30/bloomberg-completes-acquisition-of-bna.html*.

Breslin, J. (2012) "A Human Resource - BIALL Conference 2012." The BIALL Blog, March 12, 2012. Available at: *http://biall.blogspot.com/2012/03/human-resource-biall- conference-2012.html*.

British and Irish Association of Law Librarians (2011) *BIALL Salary Survey 2010/2011*. London: British and Irish Association of Law Librarians.

Butterfield, G. (2007) "Is a J.D. Necessary for Law Librarians?" LLRX.com, June 25, 2007. Available at: *http://www.llrx.com/node/1853*.

Cadmus, F. and Orndoff, L. (2009) "The AALL Biennial Salary Survey: The Law Librarian's Tool for Fair Compensation in the Best - and Worst - of Times." *AALL Spectrum*, 14 (2) (November): 24–31.

Castanias, G. (2011) "How Librarians Add Value to Their Law Firms." On Firmer Ground blog, August 3, 2011. Available at: *http://firmerground.wordpress.com/2011/08/03/how-librarians-add-value-to-their-law-firms-advice-from-greg-castanias-jones-day-library-partner/*.

Clay, T.S. and Seeger, E.A. (2012). *Law Firms in Transition: An Altman Weil Flash Survey*. Published by Altman Weil, Inc. Available at: *http://www.altmanweil.com/LFiT2012/*.

Collings, O. (2011). "LPO Movement Gains Momentum at ACLA conference." *Australasian Legal Business*, November 29, 2011. Available at: *http://au.legalbusiness online.com/site-search/lpo-movement-gains-momentum-at-acla-conference/107612*.

Coolidge, K. (2007) "Law Librarian, Private Law Firm." In Shontz, P.K. and Murray, R.A. (eds), *A Day in the Life: Career Options in Library and Information Science*. Westport, Conn: Libraries Unlimited.

Crawford, W. (2011) "Library 2.0 Five Years Later." *Online: Exploring Technology & Resources for Information Professionals*, 35 (2): 58–60.

Curle, D. (2004). "TrendAlert: Lowry's Reports v. Legg Mason – The $20 Million Copyright Wake-Up Call." Outsell's *InfoAboutInfo Briefing*, Vol. 7, April 9, 2004. Available at: *http://www.copyright.com/media/pdfs/white-paper-04-04-09.pdf*.

Davenport, C. (2012). "As Demand for E-books Soars, Libraries Struggle to Stock Their Virtual Shelves." *Washington Post*, January 14, 2012. Available at: *http://www.washingtonpost.com/local/as-demand-for-e-books-soars-libraries-struggle-to-stock-their-virtual-shelves/2012/01/13/gIQAkIOXzP_story.html*

Deloitte Consulting (2011). *The Resurgence of Corporate Legal Process Outsourcing: Leveraging a New and Improved Legal Support Business Model.* Available at: *http://www.deloitte.com/view/en_US/us/Services/additional-services/Service-Delivery-Transformation/d0fdbef1dc141310VgnVCM3000001c56f00aRCRD.htm.*

Devlin, K. (2007) "Director of Library Services, Law Firm." In Shontz, P.K. and Murray, R.A. (eds), *A Day in the Life: Career Options in Library and Information Science.* Westport, Conn: Libraries Unlimited.

Dilloff, N.J. (2011). "The Changing Cultures and Economics of Large Law Firm Practice and Their Impact on Legal Education." *Maryland Law Review*, 70: 341–363.

Downey, M. (2010) *Introduction to Law Firm Practice.* Chicago, Ill.: Law Practice Management Section, American Bar Association.

Durrant, F. (2006) "Case Study: Law Firm Libraries." In Worley, L. (ed), *BIALL Handbook of Legal Information Management.* Aldershot, Hants, England: Ashgate.

Egan, E.M. (2008) "Law Firm Librarianship: Moving Toward Harnessing Knowledge in a Changing Informational Landscape." In Aspatore Books, *The Changing Role of Law Firm Librarianship: Leading Librarians on Developing Budgets, Evaluating Resources, and Responding to the Expanding Role of the Law Firm Library.* Boston, Mass.: Thomson/Aspatore.

Empson, L. (1999) "Lessons from Professional Services Firms." *Financial Times*, November 8, 1999.

Empson L (2006), "Professionals in partnership." In J. Craig (ed.), *Production Values: Futures for Professionalism.* London: Demos. Available at: *http://www.demos.co.uk/ files/productionvalues1.pdf?1240939425.*

Flood, J. (2007) "Lawyers as Sanctifiers: The Role of Elite Law Firms in International Business Transactions." *Indiana Journal of Global Legal Studies*, 14(1): 35–66.

Frazier, K. (2001). "The Librarians' Dilemma: Contemplating the Costs of the 'Big Deal.'" *D-Lib Magazine*, 7:3 (March). Available at: *http://www.dlib.org/dlib/march01/ frazier/03frazier.html.*

Friedmann, R. (2007). "Is Offshoring the Same as Delegation?" Prism Legal blog, May 21, 2007. Available at: *http://www.prismlegal.com/wordpress/index.php? p=617&c=1*

Fronterion LLC (2011). *Ten for 2012: Top Ten Trends for Legal Outsourcing in 2012.* Available at: *http:// fronterion.com/tenfor2012/.*

Fronterion LLC (2010). "Global Sourcing 2010: AmLaw 50." Fronterion LLC, July 7, 2010. Available at: *http:// fronterion.com/amlaw-global-sourcing-2010/.*

Furlong, J. (2010). "Metamorphosis: Five Forces Transforming the Legal Services Marketplace." *Law Practice: The Business of Practicing Law*, 36(1). Available at: *http://www.americanbar.org/publications/law_ practice_home/law_practice_archive/lpm_magazine_ articles_v36_is1_pg44.html.*

Furlong, J. (2012). "Climbing the Value Ladder: Rethinking the Law Library on the Road to 2020. Discussed by Jordan Furlong, Keynote Speaker at PLL Summit." Dewey B Strategic blog, June 17, 2012. Available at: *http://deweybstrategic.blogspot.com/2012/06/climbing-value-ladder-rethinking-law.html.*

Galanter, M. and Roberts, S. (2008) "From Kinship to Magic Circle: the London Commercial Law Firm in the Twentieth Century." *International Journal of the Legal Profession*. 15(3): 143–178.

Gebauer, M. (2011). "Reinventing Librarians: Part 1." FreePint, July 1, 2011. Available to FreePint subscribers at: *http://web.freepint.com/go/sub/article/66300*.

Gediman, M. (2012). "The Business of the Law Firm Library: The Value of a Law Firm Library's Manager and Staff." *AALL Spectrum*, 16:4, 13–14. Available at: *http://www.aallnet.org/main-menu/Publications/spectrum/Vol-16/No-4/business.pdf*.

Glater, J.D. (2008). "Law Firms Feel Strain of Layoffs and Cutbacks." *New York Times*, November 11, 2008. Available at: *http://www.nytimes.com/2008/11/12/business/12law.html?pagewanted=all&_moc.semityn.www*.

Green, S. (2012). "ACC Census Sees Power, Pay, and Prestige for In-House Counsel." *Corporate Counsel*, March 30, 2012. Available at: *http://www.law.com/jsp/cc/PubArticleCC.jsp?id=1202547396614*.

Harner, M. (2011) "The Value of 'Thinking like a Lawyer'" *Maryland Law Review*, 70(2): 390–419.

Harris, L.E. (2009). *Licensing Digital Content: A Practical Guide for Librarians. 2nd edition.* Chicago: American Library Association.

Harvey, T. (2003). *The Role of the Legal Information Officer.* Oxford, UK: Chandos.

He, L., Chaudhuri, B, and Juterbock, D. (2011). "Value Creation, Assessment, and Communication in a Corporate Library." In Kelsey, S.E. and Porter, M.J. (eds.), *Best Practices for Corporate Libraries.* Santa Barbara, Calif.: Libraries Unlimited.

Heller, J.S. (2002). "Copyright, Fair Use and the For-Profit Sector." *Information Outlook*, May 2002. Available to SLA members at: *http://www.sla.org/io/backissues.cfm*.

Hildebrandt Institute and Citi Private Bank (2012). "2012 Client Advisory." Thomson Reuters, February 15, 2012. Available at: *https://peermonitor.thomsonreuters.com/ThomsonPeer/docs/2012_Client_Advisory.pdf.*

Hitt, M.A., Bierman, L. and Collins, J.D. (2007). "The Strategic Evolution of Large US Law Firms." *Business Horizons*, 50 (1): 17–28.

Ho, C. (2012). "The Fracturing of Big Law." *Washington Post*, May 13, 2012. Available at: *http://www.washingtonpost.com/business/capitalbusiness/the-fracturing-of-big-law/2012/05/11/gIQAgkNvMU_story.html*

Hodnicki, J. (2012a). "Advantage Bloomberg Law? Part 1: Not until BLaw unleashes BNA's sales force to get boots on the ground." Law Librarian Blog, February 14, 2012. Available at: *http://lawprofessors.typepad.com/law_librarian_blog/2012/02/advantage-bloomberg-law-part-1-bna-sales-force.html.*

Hodnicki, J. (2012b). "Advantage Bloomberg? Part 2: Yes, once BNA resources are fully integrated into or current BNA costs are offset for BLaw to compete with Wolters Kluwer." Law Librarian Blog, February 15, 2012. Available at: *http://lawprofessors.typepad.com/law_librarian_blog/2012/02/advantage-bloomberg-part-2-blaw-wk-competition.html.*

Hodnicki, J. (2012c). "Advantage Bloomberg? Part 3: BLaw will not become a viable primary provider until it offers 'solutions.'"Law Librarian Blog, February 16, 2012. Available at: *http://lawprofessors.typepad.com/law_librarian_blog/2012/02/advantage-bloomberg-part-3-blaw-solutions.html.*

Hodnicki, J. (2012d). "Advantage Bloomberg? Part 4: BLaw will be competitive with WEXIS as a primary provider in a solutions-driven market before the end of this decade."

Law Librarian Blog, February 17, 2012. Available at: *http://lawprofessors.typepad.com/law_librarian_ blog/2012/02/advantage-bloomberg-part-4-blaw-primary-provider-status.html*.

Holden, J. (2010). *Acquisitions in the New Information Universe: Core Competencies and Ethical Practices.* London: Facet Publishing.

Holmberg, K., Huvila, I., Kronqvist-Berg, M. and Widen-Wulff, G. (2009) "What is Library 2.0?" *Journal of Documentation,* 65 (4): 668–681.

Housewright, R. (2009). "Themes of Change in Corporate Libraries: Considerations for Academic Libraries." *portal: Libraries and the Academy,* 9 (2): 253–271.

Jones, A. (2009). "2.12.09: The Darkest Day Ever for Big Law Firms?" Law Blog, *Wall Street Journal,* February 12, 2009. Available at: *http://blogs.wsj.com/law/2009/02/ 12/21209-the-darkest-day-ever-for-big-law-firms/*.

Jones, A. (2010). "On the Lexis and Westlaw of the (Very) Near Future." Law Blog, *Wall Street Journal* January 25, 2010. Available at: *http://blogs.wsj.com/law/2010/01/25/ on-the-lexis-and-westlaw-of-the-near-future/*.

Keyes, A.M. (1995). "The Value of the Special Library: Review and Analysis." *Special Libraries,* 86 (3): 172–187. Available at: *http://www.sla.org/speciallibraries/ ISSN00386723V86N3.PDF*.

Kilroy, T. (2012). "Lies, Damn Lies and Metrics - Lawyers' Unhappy Relationship with Data." Legal Village blog, *Legal Week,* June 14, 2012. Available at: *http://www. legalweek.com/legal-week/blog-post/2184250/lies-damn-lies-metrics-lawyers-unhappy-relationship*.

Kirk, D. (2012) "What is the Value of Associations, or Is It Safe to Row Alone?" *AALL Spectrum,* 16 (4): 4.

Lambert, G. (2009) "SLA Name Remains - Comments from Texas Members." 3 Geeks and a Law Blog, December 11,

2009. Available at: *http://www.geeklawblog.com/search? q=%22SLA+Name+Remains%22*.

Lambert, G. (2012a) "Is 'Self-Help' a Good Thing Or a Bad Thing?" 3 Geeks and a Law Blog, March 27, 2012. Available at: *http://www.geeklawblog.com/2012/03/is-self-help-good-thing-bad-thing.html*.

Lambert, G. (2012b). "The 3 Foot Radius of the Law Library." 3 Geeks and a Law Blog, April 2, 2012. Available at: *http://www.geeklawblog.com/2012/04/3-foot-radius-of-law-library.html*.

Law, D. (2009) "Digital Library Economics: Aspects and Prospects." In Baker, D. and Evans, W. (eds), *Digital Library Economics: An Academic Perspective*. Oxford: Chandos.

Law Society (2011). "Legal Services Act," Last updated: 31 March 2011. Available at: *http://www.lawsociety.org.uk/currentissues/lsa.page*.

LeDoux, E. and Bohls, D. (2007) "A Day in the Life of the Covington & Burling LLP Reference Desk." *Law Library Lights* (Newsletter of the Law Librarians Society of Washington D.C.), 50:2 (Winter): 12–13. Online at: *http://www.llsdc.org/attachments/wysiwyg/232/Lights %20W2007.pdf*.

Legal Information Institute. "Tying Arrangement." Legal Information Institute, Cornell Law School. Accessed August 5, 2012. Available at: *http://www.law.cornell.edu/ wex/tying_arrangement*.

LexisNexis (2012). "LexisNexis Announces LexisNexis Digital Library." LexisNexis press release, April 24, 2012. Available at: *http://www.lexisnexis.com/media/press-release.aspx?id=1335290703893930*.

Lin, A. (2010). "Inside the Revolution." *The American Lawyer*, October 2010.

Loss, L., Seligman, J., and Paredes, T. (2006). *Securities Regulation, 4th ed.* New York : Aspen Publishers/Wolters Kluwer Law & Business.

Lowry, C. (2012). "Training as a Library Function: Some Observations from the Outside." On Firmer Ground blog, January 23, 2012. Available at: *http://firmerground. wordpress.com/2012/01/23/training-as-a-library-function-some-observations-from-the-outside/.*

Maher, M. (2006). "Financial Management: Planning and Charging." in Worley, L. (ed), *BIALL Handbook of Legal Information Management.* Aldershot, Hants, England: Ashgate.

Mann, T. (1993) *Library Research Models: A Guide to Classification, Cataloging, and Computers.* New York: Oxford.

Mann, T. (2005) *The Oxford Guide to Library Research, 3rd ed.* New York: Oxford.

Masur, D.A. (2010). "Is Legal Process Outsourcing Right for Your Company?" Mayer Brown, February 12, 2010. Available at: *http://www.mayerbrown.com/publications/ Is-Legal-Process-Outsourcing-Right-for-Your-Company-02-12-2010/.*

Matarazzo, J. and Pearlstein, T. (2011a) "Survival Lessons for Libraries: Educating Special Librarians – 'The Past Is Prologue.'" *Searcher*, 19 (2): 30–39.

Matarazzo, J. and Pearlstein, T. (2011b). "Survival Lessons for Libraries: Educating Special Librarians Part 2: In Search of a Model." *Searcher*, 19 (8): 32–41.

Matarazzo, J.M. and Prusak, L. (1990). "Valuing Corporate Libraries: A Senior Management Survey." *Special Libraries*, 81 (2): 102–110. Available at: *http://www.sla. org/speciallibraries/ISSN00386723V81N2.PDF.*

Matarazzo, J.M. and Prusak, L. (1999). "The Value of Corporate Libraries: Findings from a 1995 Survey of

Senior Management." In Matarazzo, J.M. and Connolly, S.D. (eds), *Knowledge and Special Libraries*. Boston: Butterworth-Heinemann. Originally published in 1995 by the Special Libraries Association.

Matthews, J.R. (2002). *The Bottom Line: Determining and Communicating the Value of the Special Library*. Westport, Conn.: Libraries Unlimited.

Matthews, J.R. (2003). "Determining and Communicating the Value of the Special Library." *Information Outlook*, 7 (3): 26–31. Available to SLA members at: *http://www.sla.org/io/backissues.cfm*.

Matthews, S. (2012). "Providing Non-traditional Library Services in a Law Firm: An Interview with Steve Matthews." On Firmer Ground blog, April 17, 2012. Interview with Susannah Tredwell. Available at: *http://firmerground.wordpress.com/2012/04/17/providing-non-traditional-library-services-in-a-law-firm-an-interview-with-steve-matthews/*.

Mayson, S. (2008). *Global Law Firms: A Strategy Looking for a Market?* Prepared for the Georgetown Law Center for the Study of the Legal Profession symposium, "The Future of the Global Law Firm," in Washington, DC, April 17–18, 2008. Available at: *http://www.law.georgetown.edu/academics/centers-institutes/legal-profession/documents/upload/Future-Law-Firm-Symposium-MaysonWebsiteArticle.pdf*

Miller, R. K. (2011). "Intellectual Property and the Corporate Library: Understanding Best Practices in Information Sharing in U.S. Organizations." In Kelsey, S.E. and Porter, M.J. (eds.), *Best Practices for Corporate Libraries*. Santa Barbara, Calif.: Libraries Unlimited.

Morris, T., Morris, W. and Smets, M. (2008). *Reputation and Performance in Large Law Firms*. Submitted to Academy of Management conference, Anaheim, California, August 8–13, 2008. Available at: *http://www.*

sbs.ox.ac.uk/centres/professionalservices/Documents/ Smets%20-%20Reputation%20and%20Performance% 20paper%20AOM%20FINAL.pdf.

Munneke, G.A. (2006) *Law Practice Management in a Nutshell.* St. Paul, Minn: Thomson/West.

Nichols, S.L. (2008). "Aligning Library Service Lines with Business Strategy." In *How to Manage a Law Firm Library: Leading Librarians on Providing Effective Services, Managing Costs, and Updating and Maintaining Resources.* Eagan, Minn.: Aspatore Books.

Niemeier, C. (2012). "Could BNA Content Integration with Bloomberg Law Be a Match Made in Heaven for Your Law Firm?" 3 Geeks and a Law Blog, February 5, 2012. Available at: *http://www.geeklawblog.com/2012/03/ could-bna-content-integration-with.html.*

Nonthacumjane, P. (2011) "Key Skills and Competencies of a New Generation of LIS Professionals," *IFLA Journal,* 37 (4): 280–288. Available at: *http://www.ifla.org/files/assets/ hq/publications/ifla-journal/ifla-journal-37-4_2011.pdf.*

O'Brien, D.R., Gasser, U., and Palfrey, J. (2012). *E-books in Libraries: A Briefing Document Developed in Preparation for a Workshop on E-Lending in Libraries.* Berkman Center for Internet & Society, Research Publication No. 2012–15. Available at: *http://cyber.law.harvard.edu/ publications/2012/ebooks_in_libraries.*

O'Grady, J.P. (2011). "Outsourcing, Outrage or Opportunity? What is Core?" Dewey B Strategic blog, February 25, 2011. Available at: *http://deweybstrategic.blogspot.com/ search?q=%22what+is+core%22.*

O'Grady, J.P. (2012a). "Welcome to Bloomberg Law: No Deals, No Discounts, No Apology." Dewey B Strategic blog, February 10, 2012. Available at: *http:// deweybstrategic.blogspot.com/2012/02/welcome-to- bloomberg-law-no-deals-no.html.*

O'Grady, J.P. (2012b). "Law Libraries Transformed: Crowded Collaboration and Social Solitude (The Apple Store vs. The Commons)." Dewey B Strategic blog, July 18, 2012. Available at: *http://deweybstrategic.blogspot. com/2012/07/law-libraries-transformedcrowded.html*.

Oder, N. (2009) "SLA Members Reject Name Change to ASKPro." *Library Journal*, December 10, 2009. Available at: *http://www.libraryjournal.com/article/CA6711116. html*.

Parsons, M. (2004). *Effective Knowledge Management for Law Firms*. Oxford; New York: Oxford University Press.

Partridge, H., Lee, J., and Munro, C. (2010) "Becoming 'Librarian 2.0': The Skills, Knowledge, and Attributes Required by Library and Information Science Professionals in a Web 2.0 World (and Beyond)." *Library Trends*, 59 (1–2): 315–335.

Pogrebin, R. (2012). "New York Public Library Defends Plan to Renovate." *New York Times*, April 15, 2012. Available at: *http://www.nytimes.com/2012/04/16/arts/ design/new-york-public-library-counters-critics-of-renovation-plans.html?pagewanted=all*.

Purzycki, M. (2012). "Large Law + LPO Providers = Growing Trend." The Hildebrandt Institute Blog, February 3, 2012. Available at: *http://hildebrandtblog. com/2012/02/03/large-law-lpo-providers-growing-trend/*.

Qualters, S. (2011). "Outsourcing Pioneer Brings Work Back to the U.S." *National Law Journal*, July 7, 2011.

Radin, S.A. (2009). *The Business Judgment Rule: Fiduciary Duties of Corporate Directors, 6th ed*. New York: Aspen Publishers/Wolters Kluwer Law & Business.

Rampell, C. (2011). "At Well-Paying Law Firms, a Low-Paid Corner." *New York Times*, May 23, 2011. Available at: *http://www.nytimes.com/2011/05/24/business/ 24lawyers.html?_r=3&ref=business&src=m*.

Randazzo, S. (2011). "Pillsbury to Move Back-Office Workers to Nashville." *The Am Law Daily*, October 18, 2011. Available at: *http://amlawdaily.typepad.com/amlawdaily/2011/10/pillsbury-plans-back-office-operation-in-nashville.html*.

Ring, S. (2012). "Integreon Opens First UK LPO Base and Ramps up Temp Paralegal Service." *Legal Week*, January 27, 2012.

Rink, T. (2009) "SLA's Alignment Project." Alignment Project page. Available at: *http://www.sla.org/content/SLA/alignment/index.cfm*.

Riskin, G. (2012). Quoted in "Do You Really Want to Make Partner?" by Shelley DuBois, *CNN Money*, March 26, 2012, available at: *http://management.fortune.cnn.com/2012/03/26/do-you-really-want-to-make-partner/*.

Robertson, C.B. (2011). "A Collaborative Model of Offshore Legal Outsourcing," *Arizona State Law Journal*, 43(1): 125–179.

Rusanow, G. (2003). *Knowledge Management and the Smarter Lawyer*. New York: ALM Publications.

Ryder, V.J. (2011). "Measuring Value in Corporate Libraries." In Kelsey, S.E. and Porter, M.J. (eds.), *Best Practices for Corporate Libraries*. Santa Barbara, Calif.: Libraries Unlimited.

Sachdev, A. (2011). "Growth of Legal Outsourcing May Herald Era of Cheaper Lawyering." *Los Angeles Times*, January 1, 2011. Available at: *http://articles.latimes.com/2011/jan/01/business/la-fi-legal-outsourcing-20110101*.

Saint-Onge, M. (2009) "Law Librarian 2.0: Building the Law Librarian of the Future." LexisNexis InfoPro, Librarian Relations Consultants column, March 2009. Available at: *http://law.lexisnexis.com/infopro/Librarian-Relations-Group/Meet-the-LRCs/Law-Librarian-20-Building-the-Law-Librarian-of-the-Future-0309/*.

Saw, G. and Todd, H. (2007) "Library 3.0: Where Art Our Skills?" Proceedings of the World Library and Information Congress, 73rd IFLA General Conference and Council, August 19–23, 2007. Available at: *http://archive.ifla.org/IV/ifla73/papers/151-Saw_Todd-en.pdf*.

Sears, D.S. (2006) "Vision: The Essence of Professionalism and Key to the Future of Law Librarianship as a Profession." *Law Library Journal*, 98 (1): 81–97.

Segal-Horn, S. and Dean, A. (2007). "The Globalization of Law Firms: Managerial Issues." *International Journal of Service Industry Management*, 18(2): 206–219.

Sellen, A.J. and Harper, R.H.R. (2002). *The Myth of the Paperless Office*. Cambridge, Mass.: MIT Press.

Sellers, C.L. and Gragg, P. (2012). "WestlawNext and Lexis Advance." *Law Library Journal*, 104:2. Available at: *http://www.aallnet.org/main-menu/Publications/llj/vol-104/no-2/2012-25.pdf*.

Simmons, C. (2012). "Dewey Bankruptcy Filing Raises Novel Issues." *New York Law Journal*, May 29, 2012.

Smets, M., T. Morris, Carroll, S. and N. Malhotra (2009) *Orchestrating for a Winning Performance: Re-thinking Strategy in Professional Service Firms*. Novak Druce Centre for Professional Service Firms, Said Business School, University of Oxford. Available at: *http://www.sbs.ox.ac.uk/centres/professionalservices/Documents/Smets%20-%20Orchestrating%20for%20a%20winning%20performance.pdf*.

Stemlar, A. (2008). "Providing Value in the Legal Industry Today." In Aspatore Books, *The Changing Role of Law Firm Librarianship: Leading Librarians on Developing Budgets, Evaluating Resources, and Responding to the Expanding Role of the Law Firm Library*. Boston, Mass.: Thomson/Aspatore.

Stewart, J.B. (2012). "Dewey's Fall Underscores Law Firms' New Reality." *New York Times*, May 4, 2012. Available at: *http://www.nytimes.com/2012/05/05/business/deweys-collapse-underscores-a-new-reality-for-law-firms-common-sense.html?_r=1&pagewanted=all.*

Strouse, R. (2003). "Demonstrating Value and Return on Investment: The Ongoing Imperative." *Information Outlook*, 7 (3): 14–19. Available to SLA members at: *http://www.sla.org/io/backissues.cfm.*

Summers, N. (2011). "Bloomberg's Plan for World Domination." *The Daily Beast*, November 21, 2011. Available at: *http://www.thedailybeast.com/newsweek/2011/11/20/bloomberg-s-plan-for-world-domination.html.*

Svengalis, K.F. (2011). "Globalisation and Commercial Legal Publishing." In Danner, R.A. and Winterton, J. (eds.), *The IALL International Handbook of Legal Information Management.* Surrey, UK: Ashgate.

Sykes, J. (2003). "Value as Calculation and Value as Contribution to the Organization." *Information Outlook*, 7 (3): 10–13. Available to SLA members at: *http://www.sla.org/io/backissues.cfm.*

Taylor, A.G. and Joudrey, D.N. (2008) *The Organization of Information, 3rd edition.* Westport, Conn: Libraries Unlimited.

Thomson Reuters (2010). "Thomson Reuters Acquires Pangea3." Company press release, November 18, 2010. Available at: *http://thomsonreuters.com/content/press_room/legal/318316.*

Timmons, H. (2011). "Legal Outsourcing Firms Creating Jobs for American Lawyers." *New York Times*, June 2, 2011. Available at: *http://www.nytimes.com/2011/06/03/business/03reverse.html?_r=3&nl=todaysheadlines&adxnnl=1&adxnnlx=1338049419-cvU88e7KCz4NWd6oAlB1bA.*

Von Nordenflycht, A. (2010). "What is a Professional Service Firm? Towards a Theory and Taxonomy of

Knowledge Intensive Firms." *Academy of Management Review*, 35:1, 155–174

Waremath, L. and Kaczorowski, M.M. (2008). "Cost Recovery: A Team Effort." *Legal Management*, 27:5, 25–31.

Webster, P.M. (2008). *Managing Electronic Resources: New and Changing Roles for Libraries*. Oxford: Chandos.

Welch, E.P., Turezyn, A.J., and Saunders, R.S. (2012). *Folk on the Delaware General Corporation Law, 5th ed.* New York: Aspen Publishers/Wolters Kluwer Law & Business.

Wenig, J. (2007). "First listing heralds change." *Australian Financial Review*, May 25, 2007, First Edition, pg. 58.

Wheeler, R.E. (2011). "Does WestlawNext Really Change Everything? The Implications of WestlawNext on Legal Research." *Law Library Journal*, 103:3. Available at: *http://www.aallnet.org/main-menu/Publications/llj/LLJ-Archives/Vol-103/2011-03/2011-23.pdf*.

White, H.S. (1979). "Cost-Effectiveness and Cost-Benefit Determinations in Special Libraries." *Special Libraries*, 70 (4): 163–169. Available at: *http://www.sla.org/speciallibraries/ISSN00386723V70N4.PDF*.

Will, L. (2008) "Librarianship: A Profession in Transition." In Aspatore Books, *The Changing Role of Law Firm Librarianship: Leading Librarians on Developing Budgets, Evaluating Resources, and Responding to the Expanding Role of the Law Firm Library*. Boston, Mass.: Thomson/Aspatore.

Woldring. E. (2001). "Strategies to Measure the Value of Special Libraries." *Australian Law Librarian*, 9 (4): 284–295.

Index

CPSIA information can be obtained at www.ICGtesting.com
Printed in the USA
LVOW100711220213

321198LV00002B/24/P

9 781843 347088